Sue

GOD'S

SUPERNATURAL

POWER

You will See God's
Power
Psa. 90:16-17

GOD'S
SUPERNATURAL
POWER

Bobby Conner

DESTINY IMAGE₀ PUBLISHERS, INC.
P.O. Box 310, Shippensburg, PA 17257-0310

*"Speaking to the Purposes of God for this
Generation and for the Generations to Come."*

This book and all other Destiny Image, Revival Press, Mercy Place, Fresh Bread, Destiny Image Fiction, and Treasure House books are available at Christian bookstores and distributors worldwide.

For a U.S. bookstore nearest you, call 1-800-722-6774.
For more information on foreign distributors, call 717-532-3040.
Or reach us on the Internet: www.destinyimage.com.

ISBN 10: 0-7684-2498-4
ISBN 13: 978-0-7684-2498-0

For Worldwide Distribution, Printed in the U.S.A.

1 2 3 4 5 6 7 8 9 10 11 / 09 08 07

Endorsements

Every believer desires to have a greater understanding of the anointing of the Holy Spirit and to move more effectively in the spirit realm. I know few who can do this as wisely and sensitively as Bobby Conner. His book, *God's Supernatural Power*, is a great tool to help us accomplish this. Power, character, and truth are molded together in this dynamic Christ-centered book.

Mahesh Chavda

Bobby Conner's *God's Supernatural Power* is a gripping account of transformation, regeneration, and the power to become all God created you to be. However we view ourselves that is not in agreement with the way God sees us is a mental stronghold. The Bible states that these mental strongholds exalt themselves against the knowledge of God, in this case His knowledge of us and the purpose for which He created us.

This book is sure to change how you view the reason He made you.

John Paul Jackson

From the first day I met him, Bobby Conner has been a mouthpiece and conduit of God's supernatural power. I have observed first-hand his prophetic accuracy and desperate heart-longing after the person of Jesus. It is with whole-hearted confidence and support that I recommend his book, *God's Supernatural Power*. This generation stands on the threshold of the greatest demonstration of God's power ever witnessed on the earth. Many people are being prepared to steward notable mantels of revelation and power. Bobby's book will help facilitate the preparatory process and position many of today's believers to apprehend this fresh impartation of God's grace and favor.

Paul Keith Davis
Founder, WhiteDove Ministries

God's Supernatural Power is a clarion call to divine encounters with the Living God. Bobby's desire to see a generation rise up and embrace their unique destiny is challenging and refreshing. Also typical of Bobby's heart is the fatherly encouragement that is expressed throughout the pages of this manuscript. I recommend you read this book over and over again! It will encourage you and change your life!

Larry Randolph

Few people that I know are as qualified to write a book on the supernatural as is Bobby Conner. His lifestyle is a constant reminder of what God can do through a yielded vessel. Every time I'm with Bobby, I leave stirred up and hungry for more. And now we have his insights and stories in a book. I highly recommend *God's Supernatural Power*, knowing it will have a radical impact on your life!

Bill Johnson

Bobby Conner is a gentle giant, a dear friend, and a true Papa in the prophetic. In *God's Supernatural Power*, Bobby Conner lays a firm and thorough foundation in the Word to catapult you into your destiny. The greatest battle field is in our minds, and Bobby's teaching shines light into the darkness of the enemy's lies. His revelation will be "a lamp to your feet and a light to your path" (Ps. 119:105). We joyfully recommend this book for those who want to walk in God's supernatural power. Enjoy!

Dr. Heidi and Rolland Baker
Founding Directors Iris Ministries
Mozambique, Africa

God's Supernatural Power will stir you to dive deeper into the things of the Lord. With great pleasure, I highly recommend this book by Bobby Conner. Bobby is truly a man after God's own heart and a friend of God. Bobby's insight and revelation will release those who are hungry into a deeper place in Him and help them to see the impossible become possible in day-to-day living. Get ready to receive fresh revelation that releases fresh anointing from the Lord as you dive into this book. Bobby's ministry and friendship have had a great impact on my life and my whole family. We have seen first-hand the supernatural power of God flow mightily through Bobby in our conferences and meetings. Countless lives have been powerfully impacted during these meetings, and I know that you will be impacted in a great way also as you read this book.

Keith Miller
Stand Firm World Ministries

Bobby Conner clearly sees the dangers the believer faces when it comes to the issues of the heart. Since the "issues of life" flow out of the believer's heart, Bobby prophetically zooms in on the priority and importance we should give to guarding "this treasure in earthen vessels" we cherish. In his unique style, Bobby encourages but also warns us in the steps we can take to insure this treasure remains safe.

Marc Lawson
Church at North Gate/Mighty Warrior Ministries

Table of Contents

CHAPTER I

Identity Crisis

One evening, as I pulled into the parking lot of the church where I was to speak, I noticed a bunch of young people gathered in a group outside the building, vivacious, laughing, jumping around and having a great time together, as teenagers tend to do. Their lively spirit was very appealing, and I immediately felt drawn to them. I wanted to go over and talk with them and join in with their fun for a little while. But then I noticed, off to the side, another teenager, a young lady who was by herself. Somewhat overweight and wearing thick glasses, she looked very despondent and obviously did not feel she was part of the group. All at once, my intention to join the cluster of kids was arrested when I heard the Lord say to me, "Go over and speak to her."

So I walked over to her, and as I approached the Lord gave me a prophetic word for her. I said to her, "Honey, God is going to give you the power and ability to write a book."

Just for a moment her eyes lit up and a great ray of hope spread across her face. Then, even as I watched, doubt, like a dark cloud, covered her face again and she looked just as despondent as before.

Several months later, I returned to that same church and that same young lady met me at the front with her mother. She was elated and had in her hand a letter from the governor of the state, along with a newspaper article reporting that she had won first place in the state for a short story she had written and submitted. Now she was an integral part of the youth group, writing plays, skits, and scripts for them to perform. She was starting to come into her own.

By the standards of the world (and, unfortunately, of far too many churches and youth groups), she was not one of the "beautiful people," but she was beautiful to God. Where some people might have seen a "plain Jane," God saw a precious jewel with a bright and promising future. And He told her so.

In a few short months, she had changed from a "nobody" (in her own eyes) to a "somebody" with purpose and destiny. In God's eyes, of course, she had always been a "somebody"—she just didn't know it. Not, at least, until that day when, through me, God spoke a word to her that opened her eyes to who she really was.

"Who Do You Think You Are?"

This young lady's dilemma is not unique and is not limited to young people. Saints of all ages struggle daily with their spiritual identity. They are as mixed up as a termite in a yo-yo, tossed to and fro with no idea who they are in Christ and little or no scriptural knowledge to give them a solid foundation. Such ignorance in a child of God is not only tragic but also dangerous. God says, "My people are destroyed for lack of knowledge" (Hos. 4:6a). The apostle Peter warns us to, "Be sober, be vigilant; because your adversary the devil walks about like a roaring lion, seeking whom he may devour. Resist him, steadfast in the faith..." (1 Pet. 5:8-9a). Satan loves to pounce on immature believers who lack knowledge, because if he can keep them in the dark as to who they really are, he can prevent them from fulfilling their divine destiny.

God is not the author of confusion (see 1 Cor. 14:33). He desires for us to know His plans and purposes for our lives. Satan, the accuser of the brethren and the mortal enemy of our souls, is a thief and a liar who is always busy seeking to rob believers of their true identity in Christ. Ignorance leads to bondage, while the road to freedom is paved with truth. Jesus said, "You shall know the truth and the truth shall make you free" (John 8:32). The first truth we need to know is the truth of who Christ is. Second, we need to know who we are in Christ.

Heaven and hell are posing the same question to every person in the Body of Christ. The Spirit of God and the devil alike are asking us, "Who do you think you are?" It is an apt question, and the eternal destiny of millions rides on the answer. Without question, the Body of Christ today is in an identity crisis of unprecedented proportions. If we are to fulfill our spiritual destiny, we first must know who we are. But before we can discover who we are, we must comprehend who Christ is, because it is only in relation to Him that we can understand our true spiritual identity. God created us in His image (see Gen. 1:27) and has "predestined" all believers "to be conformed to the image of His Son" (Rom. 8:29). But what is the image of His Son, Jesus Christ? Paul gives us the answer: "He is the image of the invisible God, the firstborn over all creation" (Col. 1:15), in whom "dwells all the fullness of the Godhead bodily" (Col. 2:9). And God wants to make us just like Him!

Even though we each are made in God's image, He also made each of us unique. God delights to display Himself in our individuality. He loves diversity. Every leaf on every tree is different from every other leaf. Every snowflake is different from every other snowflake. God even gave each of us our own personal and absolutely unique set of fingerprints.

There is no one else in the entire world like you. You are one of a kind by divine design. God created you to be uniquely you and endowed you with particular gifts, talents, and abilities so that you can fill your unique place in His plan and fulfill your destiny in life. No one else can do what God has called and equipped you to do—no one. Somebody said, "God don't make no junk." Well, I've got news for you: God don't make no clones, either! There are no copies of you anywhere in the world, and that's just the way God wants it.

The world hates nonconformists. It will try to shape you into its own cookie-cutter pattern so that you look and sound and act like everybody else. Don't let that happen! You are too precious to God and too important to the Body of Christ to allow your uniqueness to be squeezed out. Paul said, "Do not be conformed to this world, but be transformed by the renewing of your mind, that you may prove what is that good and acceptable and perfect will of God" (Rom. 12:2). One modern English paraphrase of this verse really gets the idea across: "Don't let the world around you squeeze you into its own mould, but let God re-make you so that your whole attitude of mind is changed. Thus you will prove in practice that the will of God's good, acceptable to Him and perfect" (Rom. 12:2 Phillips). Rejoice in who you are—the person God made you—and don't worry about trying to be somebody you were not created to be.

Somebody might be saying, "That may be fine for you, but I'm not an eloquent preacher or a talented musician. I can't teach, and I'm shy around people I don't know. I'm nobody special." God disagrees! The world may look at you that way, but God judges by a different standard. While the world pursues "superstars," God searches for people who are hungry for Him, ordinary folks through whom He can do extraordinary things. Where the world judges by external appearances, God looks at the heart (see 1 Sam. 16:7). So if your heart is right, if you are hungry for God, He not only can use you, He wants to use you!

But it won't happen unless you believe it. Until you stop listening to what the world says about you and start listening to what God says about you, you will never realize your full identity in Christ or fulfill the destiny God has for you. It all boils down to how you think, to what the Phillips translation of Romans 12:2 calls an "attitude of mind." For the mind is where the battle for your destiny (and mine) is fought. That is why Paul insists that we must have our minds renewed, which calls for a complete transformation of our thinking. We must learn to lay aside the worldly mind-set and take up the "mind of Christ" (see 1 Cor. 2:16).

One definition of *destiny* is, "the inner purpose of a life that can be discovered and realized." Discovering your divine destiny and realizing (accomplishing) what God has called you to achieve is the most important thing you could ever do. It's what you were born for. Renewing your mind, transforming your thinking from the world's point of view to God's perspective, will enable to fulfill your destiny. A renewed mind will aid you in carrying out Paul's instructions to "put on the new man who is renewed in knowledge according to the image of Him who created him" (Col. 3:10).

When you received Christ as your personal Savior, a great spiritual transaction took place: you received a brand new heart. At the moment of your conversion, God placed within you a changed heart, a transformed heart that made you capable of fully following His will. God says in Ezekiel, "I will give you a new heart and put a new spirit within you; I will take the heart of stone out of your flesh and give you a heart of flesh" (Ezek. 36:26). A heart of stone is a dead heart, but a heart of flesh is vibrant with life.

Proverbs 4:23 says, "Keep your heart with all diligence, for out of it spring the issues of life." In other words, as your heart goes, so goes your destiny. You can't fulfill your destiny until you know who you are, and in order to know who you are, you have to have your head on straight.

Getting Your Head on Straight

In the battlefield of our minds, the devil seeks to sow evil seeds of doubt about God, His love, and His character. At the same time, he seeks to overwhelm our spirits with mind-gripping fear. The adversary of our souls is unrelenting in his attacks on God and His Word. Satan's very first words to mankind, as recorded in Genesis chapter 3, was when he asked Eve, "Has God indeed said, 'You shall not eat of every tree of the garden'?" So very subtly, Satan sowed a seed of doubt in Eve's mind that suggested that God was holding out on her. The devil continues to use that same strategy today. He casts shadows of doubt in our minds regarding the certainty of the Word and the heart of God in an effort to make us think that God is not playing straight with us. The goodness and integrity of God should never be in doubt: "The Lord is good, a stronghold in the day of trouble; and He knows those who trust in Him" (Nah. 1:7); "Oh, taste and see that the Lord is good; blessed is the man who trusts in Him" (Ps. 37:8).

Our minds set the course and direction for our whole lives: "For as he thinks in his heart, so is he" (Prov. 23:7a). This being the case, it is vitally important that we fill our minds with the promises of God, such as Micah 3:8: "But truly I am full of power by the Spirit of the Lord, and of justice and might..." and 2 Timothy 1:7: "For God has not given us a spirit of fear, but of power and of love and of a sound mind."

So what is the key to getting your head on straight? Fill your mind with the right kind of thoughts. Think about the right kind of things, as Paul says:

> *Finally, brethren, whatever things are true, whatever things are noble, whatever things are just, whatever things are pure, whatever things are lovely, whatever things are of good report, if there is any virtue and if there is anything praiseworthy—meditate on these things* (Philippians 4:8).

My high school football coach taught me a principle to aid me in bringing down the ball carrier: "The body will always follow the head." The same is true in our spiritual lives. If our minds are filled with wrong desires, we will waste our lives trying to satisfy them. On the other hand, if we set high and noble standards for thought and life, God will help us meet them because, "The steps of a good man are ordered by the Lord, and He delights in his way" (Ps. 37:23). We can achieve this upright life only by yielding control of our lives to the Holy Spirit. This requires that we die to self, self-will, and self-rule so that we can live to God, an act that Paul calls a "living sacrifice": "I beseech you therefore, brethren, by the mercies of God, that you present your bodies a living sacrifice, holy, acceptable to God, which is your reasonable service" (Rom. 12:1).

Our hearts, minds, and spirits will never be free as long as we think and walk according to the flesh. We will realize our freedom in Christ only as we learn to walk by the Spirit of God. As Paul assures us: "There is therefore now no condemnation to those who are in Christ Jesus, who do not walk according to the flesh, but according to the Spirit. For the law of the Spirit of life in Christ Jesus has made me free from the law of sin and death" (Rom. 8:1-2); and: "I say then: walk in the Spirit, and you shall not fulfill the lust of the flesh" (Gal. 5:16). If you allow the Holy Spirit to guide your thoughts and your steps, He will bring great grace to your life. Only then will you be truly free to become all that God has purposed you to be.

If we are going to change our lifestyles, we must first change our mind-sets. We need a true "brain washing" in order to rid ourselves of "stinking thinking." Our minds need to be thoroughly cleansed of the lies and filth of the world so that we can take up the mind of Christ, learning to think as He thinks and to see as He sees. A cleansed and renewed mind will completely change our perception of life and the world around us.

The Spirit of God is calling each of us to a higher standard, to "walk worthy of the Lord, fully pleasing Him, being fruitful in every good work and increasing in the knowledge of God" (Col. 1:10). This is not a season to be at ease and loose about our lifestyle. We must pursue peace and holiness, for without them we will not see the Lord (see Heb. 12:14). God calls all of His people to a life of purity, which is the path to holiness. As Paul writes, "Therefore, having these promises, beloved, let us cleanse ourselves from all filthiness of the flesh and spirit, perfecting holiness in the fear of God" (2 Cor. 7:1). This is a call to our complete consecration, in both body and spirit.

In other words, we must figuratively lay down bodies and spirits as living sacrifices on the altar of God. Leviticus 1:8 describes the process for consecrating a "voluntary offering" brought to the Lord by the people. The entire sacrificial animal—"the parts, the head and the fat"—was laid on the altar and burned completely. The fact that the animal's head was laid on the altar is significant for us because it reminds us that our minds must also be surrendered to the Lord for cleansing and consecrating, which is symbolized by the fire of the offering. It is with clean, consecrated minds that we enter into communion with the Lord.

A closer look at Leviticus 1:8 reveals several prophetic insights: "Then the priests, Aaron's sons, shall lay the parts, the head, and the fat in order on the wood that is on the fire upon the altar." The name *Aaron* depicts "those who lift the light." Accordingly, we are called to be the light of the world, a city set upon a high hill that cannot be hidden (see Matt. 5:14). The sacrificial animal was to be laid on the wood on the fire of the altar. It is only as the fire of God's Spirit falls upon us that we are truly empowered. In Acts chapter 2, the tongues of fire rested upon the heads of all in the upper room, and each one was filled with the Holy Spirit and with power.

There is an old gospel hymn that says:

> Is your all on the altar of sacrifice laid?
> Your heart, does the Spirit control?
> You can only be blest and have peace and sweet rest,
> As you yield Him your body and soul.

It is time for us to lay our all on the altar and embrace the holy fire of God's presence! We must present a mind that is clean and wholly consecrated to Him. Like David, our cry must be: "Create in me a clean heart, O God, and renew a steadfast spirit within me" (Ps. 51:10). When we do, we will discover that the Lord is transforming our worldly minds into spiritual minds—His mind.

The Spiritual Mind

In the second chapter of his first letter to the Corinthians, the apostle Paul contrasts the natural mind and the spiritual mind. The natural mind, corrupted by sin, is dulled and darkened to spiritual things, however brilliant it may be in its own natural sphere. There are many intellectually brilliant people who haven't a clue regarding spiritual realities. They are "always learning and never able to come to the knowledge of the truth" (2 Tim. 3:7). Paul goes so far as to say that it is impossible for the natural mind to comprehend the things of the Spirit: "But the natural man does not receive the things of the Spirit of God, for they are foolishness to him; nor can he know them, because they are spiritually discerned" (1 Cor. 2:14). It takes a spiritual mind to comprehend spiritual truth.

As contradictory as it may seem, many true children of God are dominated still, for the most part, by the laws of their natural or carnal mind. One of the reasons the Church struggles so much today is because so many Christians still think like the world. And thoughts give birth to actions. Some say, for example, "I won't believe it until I see it." This is the exact opposite to the spiritual mind. Jesus declared, "Did I not say to you that if you would believe you would see the glory of God?" (John 11:40). He spoke these words at the tomb of Lazarus in response to Martha's warning of the stench that would result if the tomb was opened as He had requested. Martha was looking and thinking from a carnal perspective. Jesus changed her viewpoint by raising her brother from the dead.

The natural mind says, "If I see, I will believe." The spiritual mind says, "If I believe, I will see." Paul clearly recognized our desperate need for Spirit-enlightened minds, praying

> that the God of our Lord Jesus Christ, the Father of glory, may give to you the Spirit of wisdom and revelation in the knowledge of Him, the eyes of your understanding being enlightened; that you may know what is the hope of His calling, what are the riches of the glory of His inheritance in the saints (Ephesians 1:17-18).

Only in His light can we see light. We should cry out to God for spiritual eyes to see what we believe, even as we seek each day to walk in the light of His revealed Word.

No matter how intellectually brilliant we may be, we cannot understand even the simplest concepts of God without the enlightenment of the Holy Spirit. The knowledge of spiritual things does not come by intellectual effort. Rather, it comes only by divine revelation. This is why, when Peter declared to Jesus, "You are the Christ, the Son of the living God," Jesus said to him, "Blessed are you, Simon Bar-Jonah, for flesh and blood has not revealed this to you, but My Father who is in Heaven" (Matt. 16:16-17).

God's desire for all of His children is that they possess and use a spiritual mind. That capacity already resides in each of us through the indwelling Holy Spirit. What Jesus said to His disciples applies also to us: "Blessed are your eyes for they see, and your ears for they hear" (Matt. 13:16). Do you want to cultivate your spiritual mind? Then immerse yourself in the Word of God. Pray for revelation. Ask the Spirit of God to open your eyes to behold awesome things from God. There is nothing wrong with intellectual knowledge and pursuit. God gave us our minds and expects us to use them. However, we should never depend upon our mere human intellectual wisdom to advance us in the realm of the Holy Spirit. It is the humble, spiritually-minded person of childlike faith to whom God imparts great grace and upon whom He releases a powerful anointing.

God's Way Up Is Down

Beside the fact that God gives grace to the humble, another motivating factor for walking in true humility is that it is the steppingstone for launching you into deeper revelation. Genuinely humble people receive wisdom and insight from God that are withheld from those who are proud, arrogant, or wise in their own eyes. Such honor shown to the humble made Jesus rejoice: "At that time Jesus answered and said, 'I thank You, Father, Lord of Heaven and earth, that You have hidden these things from the wise and prudent and have revealed them to babes'" (Matt. 11:25). The word *babes* here has nothing to do with chronological age but refers to spiritual attitude and maturity. God resists the proud but pours out His grace and favor on all who approach Him with the open-hearted faith of a child. They are the ones to whom God reveals His greatest secrets.

Actually, God calls ordinary people and anoints them with an extraordinary anointing to accomplish outstanding displays of His power. Why? So that He will be the one who receives the glory. When people see amazing, God-like things taking place in and through the lives of "ordinary" folks, they will know that God is at work and will glorify Him. Where are all the "superstar saints" in the Bible? There are none. Just take a look at every Bible hero. In every case—in every case—God took ordinary "nobodies" and did extraordinary things in and through them. What made them great? Two things: 1), the powerful anointing and presence of God on their lives and 2), their humble and obedient re-sponse to God through childlike faith.

Notice that we are to be childlike, not childish. We are not talking about immaturity here but rather a tender heart and a gentle, humble, and teachable spirit. Some of the most power-ful expressions of faith today are coming from small children. I am continually amazed at the overwhelming presence of Christ being manifested in the lives of children around the world. Many of them even are moving in awesome miracles and signs and wonders. I see it everywhere I go.

Like children, we must come trusting totally in the faith-fulness of our heavenly Father, confident that He desires better for us than we could ever desire for ourselves. God loves us and always has our very best interests in mind. He said so Himself: "'For I know the thoughts that I think to-ward you,' says the Lord, 'thoughts of peace and not of evil, to give you a future and a hope'" (Jer. 29:11). Isn't it overwhelming to know that God thinks about us—that He thinks about you personally—and that His thoughts toward you are thoughts of peace, hope, and a bright future? God cares about every step you take and everything you do. He cares deeply about your every hurt, fear, joy, and sorrow. He cares about your dreams because He gave them to you and wants to see you realize them.

One day God spoke these very encouraging words to me: "My people are about to believe what they know." The Spirit of God is going to move the Word of God from our heads to our hearts and to our hands. We will become doers of the Word and not just hearers (see James 1:22).

With this in mind, it is high time to let go and let the Holy Spirit have total control of your life! Don't worry about letting go. God has more power to direct your life than the devil does to deceive you. As John assures us, "You are of God, little children, and have overcome them, because He who is in you is greater than he who is in the world" (1 John 4:4). The word *them* in the verse refers to false prophets who are filled with the spirit of antichrist. If you are a genuine believer and follower of Jesus Christ, the Holy Spirit of God indwells you and is ready to release in you the power to live the Christian life, bear witness to Christ, and manifest the glory of God as never before. Jesus Himself promised, "You shall receive power when the Holy Spirit has come upon you; and you shall be witnesses to Me in Jerusalem, and in all Judea and Samaria, and to the end of the earth" (Acts 1:8).

Daniel 11:32 tells us that it is the people who truly know God who display strength and take action. Is it any wonder, then, that the devil takes his stand and fights against us so viciously? He knows who we are. Even more, he knows who we are becoming in Christ, and it terrifies him! Have you ever thought about the fact that the devil is scared of you because you are a child of God? He is, but that doesn't mean you should try to take him on one-on-one. In that kind of match-up, you will lose every time. Remember James's admonition: "Therefore submit to God. Resist the devil and he will flee from you" (James 4:7). It is only as you submit yourself to God in humble, childlike faith that He empowers you to resist the devil so successfully that he flees.

Let your quest be to so completely yield your mind to the illumination of the Holy Spirit that your whole way of looking at things is completely transformed. The Christian life is much more than doctrine and theology. Those things are important because we need to know what we believe and why, but apart from practical application, they are little more than intellectual knowledge. The Christian life is thoroughly practical. The Christian life is theology and doctrine in action. It is truth in action. It is love in action. The Christian life is the Word of God and the power of God together in action, in and through us on a daily basis, to bring in the Lord's harvest.

The key to all this is to have a spiritual mind that has been renewed in Christ. Look to God to guide your way with His revelatory light. Let His Word be a lamp to your feet and a light to your path (see Ps. 119:105). Why stumble around in the dark when you can walk in the light? Why muddle around in a mental fog when you can have the mind of Christ? Time is short. The harvest is plentiful. And everything is now ready. God is doing a new thing in the earth. Stop listening to the lies of the devil and the life-limiting rhetoric of the world. Don't conform to this world but be transformed by the renewing of your mind through the Holy Spirit. Get rid of your identity crisis. Accept who you are—a precious child of God! Embrace who you are meant to be—an anointed vessel of God, an ordinary guy or gal through whom God wants to do extraordinary things!

CHAPTER 2

Season of the Open Book

God is doing something new and extraordinary in the earth. He is always doing extraordinary things—things only He can do—but the awesome thing about God is that He almost always uses ordinary people to do them. That means you and me and just about anyone you know. You don't have to be a superstar (thank the Lord!) but you do have to be willing to draw close to God and to let Him draw close to you.

One day the Lord said to me, "Tell my people that I shout my truths but whisper my secrets." Anybody has access to God's truths; the Bible is full of them. But only a few—those who are willing to get close—will learn His secrets. James 4:8 says, "Draw near to God and He will draw near to you...." You have to be close to hear a whisper, and secrets are reserved for intimate friends. The Lord is looking for friends, for people who are passionate enough toward Him to do whatever it takes to build the kind of relationship where they can put their ear near to His lip. Jesus said, "You are My friends if you do whatever I command you. No longer do I call you servants, for a servant does not know what his master is doing; but I have called you friends, for all things that I heard from My Father I have made known to you" (John 15:14-15).

Too often, as Christians, we think of ourselves merely as servants of the Lord. And this is true; we are servants. Even Peter, Paul, James, John, and the other apostles referred to themselves as bondservants and even slaves of Christ. We are Christ's bondservants because we belong to Him spiritually just as completely as slaves of old belonged to their masters physically. Yet Christ invites us to become so much more than just servants. He invites us to move in closer, beyond servanthood and into the intimacy of friendship with Him. Servants are told only as much and move only as close as necessary to do their jobs. They never really get to know their master. There is always a certain distance between them. But friends bare their hearts and confide secrets and confidences to one another.

Don't you want to be the Lord's friend? Some believers don't. The very thought of getting too close to God scares them. Like the ancient Israelites, who refused to come close to Mount Sinai for fear of God (see Ex. 20:18-19), these timid believers would rather stay at a "safe" distance and satisfy themselves with merely a casual acquaintance. I hope you are not one of them. Think about it: the King of the universe is not satisfied with just being your Savior and Lord—He also wants to be your friend, and He wants you to be His. How awesome is that?

God is doing a new thing in the earth. We live today in the midst of the greatest manifestation of miracles, signs, and wonders since Pentecost—and this is just the beginning! Ecclesiastes 3:1 says, "To everything there is a season, a time for every purpose under Heaven." The greatest need of the Church in this hour is for believers everywhere to get in touch with the times in order to understand what God is doing in this season. We need the anointing that rested upon the sons of Issachar, "who had understanding of the times, to know what Israel ought to do" (1 Chron. 12:32). Like them, we need to know what we, as God's people, should be doing in our day. Jesus said that He did nothing except what He saw His Father doing (see John 5:19), and that's the way we should be. We have to find out what God is doing and partner with Him in doing it. This means getting our lives "in sync" with God—synchronizing our wills to His will and our hearts to His heart. But to know His will and His heart, we must get close to Him. Knowledge of the intimate secrets and workings of God are reserved for the friends of God. As the psalmist says, "The secret [of the sweet, satisfying companionship] of the Lord have they who fear—revere and worship—Him, and He will show them His covenant, and reveal to them its [deep, inner] meaning" (Ps. 25:14 AMP).

It's Time for the Church to Power Up!

One of the curses of the modern day Church is misdiagnosis. Like the church of Laodicea (see Rev. 3:14-22), we think we are rich, wealthy, and in need of nothing while God sees us as "wretched, miserable, poor, blind, and naked" (Rev. 3:17b). We need somebody to open our eyes to the truth. We cannot continue in deception. We must know the truth so that the truth can set us free. In this season, God is going to bring us into a real, deeper understanding of our inheritance.

Listen folks, we talk a lot about Jesus, but many of us don't really know Him that well. We know a lot of facts, but not a lot of reality. God is going to change that. He is going to move from our heads to our hearts and to our hands. We're going to start believing what we know. The Word of God is absolutely central to everything we are and do as believers, but Christianity is supposed to be more than just talk. Paul said, "The kingdom of God is not in word but in power" (1 Cor. 4:20). The missing element in the Church of our day is the regular demonstration of who God is. We can preach up a storm and teach up a tempest, but people need more than just hearing our words. They also need to see the power of God revealed in our lives. Hebrews 11:1 says, "Faith is the substance of things hoped for, the evidence of things not seen." One reason so many people write off the Church as irrelevant and out of touch is because, when they look at us, they see "a form of godliness" with no power (see 2 Tim. 3:5). Talk is cheap; evidence persuades. And the evidence needed to persuade the world is the power of God manifested in the lives of His people.

We just came through a season of the open door. Now we are in a season of the open book. Christ has extended to the Church of our day the same invitation He offered the Laodiceans so long ago: "Behold, I stand at the door and knock. If anyone hears My voice and opens the door, I will come in to him and dine with him, and he with Me" (Rev. 3:20). Many of us, hungry for deeper fellowship and communion with Him, opened the door to let Him in. The door is open; now He invites us to into the season of the open book: "After these things I looked, and behold, a door standing open in Heaven. And the first voice which I heard was like a trumpet speaking with me, saying, 'Come up here, and I will show you things which must take place after this'" (Rev. 4:1). We opened the door of our hearts and our churches to Him, and He has opened the door of Heaven to us.

This season of the open book is a season of revelatory truth, the unveiling of hidden mysteries. God wants to reveal His mystic mysteries and sacred secrets to His children—mysteries that have been concealed for ages. He concealed them so we would not run with them prematurely, but I believe the time for their unveiling is at hand! They were shut up until the endtimes, until the proper season, and I believe that season is now!

The Book of Revelation is a book of unveiling; that's what the word *revelation* means. It is an uncovering of something that was hidden. One of the great messages of Revelation is the encouragement it gives to "over-comers," those who persevere in the faith. The Lord is offering to His people now the anointing of the over-comer. We will be known either as the generation that over comes or the generation that was over come. Each of the seven messages from Christ to the seven churches in Revelation chapters 2 and 3 ends with a promise to those who overcome. I want to focus on one of those promises, given to the church at Pergamos. Jesus said,

> *He who has an ear, let him hear what the Spirit says to the churches. To him who overcomes I will give some of the hidden manna to eat. And I will give him a white stone, and on the stone a new name written which no one knows except him who receives it* (Revelation 2:17b).

The Sealed Book Has Been Opened

Notice that the Lord promises two things to each over-comer: hidden manna to eat and a white stone with a new name that only the person receiving it knows. Let's consider the hidden manna first.

Manna, of course, was the food from Heaven that God provided for the Israelites during their forty years in the wilderness. It formed in the night with the dew and was "fine as frost on the ground" (Exod. 16:14), and "was like white coriander seed, and the taste of it was like wafers made with honey" (Exod. 16:31). The word *manna* means "what is it?" and that's exactly what the Israelites said when they saw it for the first time: "What is it?" The answer is simple: it was what God provided.

Jesus said that over-comers would eat hidden manna. God is revealing things to our generation that have been sealed and concealed from prior generations. Saints in those days wanted to see them. They longed to see them and to understand them, but it was not for them to know. Theirs was not the season for unveiling these things. But in the Lord's timing, we have moved into a season where that which has been concealed is now being revealed.

Daniel received prophecy that he was told to seal up and conceal until a later day: "But you, Daniel, shut up the words, and seal the book until the time of the end; many shall run to and fro, and knowledge shall increase" (Dan. 12:4). What happened to that sealed book? Where is it hidden? In the Father's right hand! According to Scripture, Father God Himself has had this book clutched in His own strong right hand: "And I saw in the right hand of Him who sat on the throne a scroll written inside and on the back, sealed with seven seals" (Rev. 5:1).

The book, or scroll, was sealed with seven seals. Seven is the number of completeness. So the book was completely, perfectly, securely sealed until the right time—and the right person appeared to unseal it. John, the recorder of this vision, continues to relate what he saw:

> *Then I saw a strong angel proclaiming with a loud voice, "Who is worthy to open the scroll and to loose its seals?" And no one in Heaven or on the earth or under the earth was able to open the scroll, or to look at it. So I wept much, because no one was found worthy to open and read the scroll, or to look at it. But one of the elders said to me, "Do not weep. Behold, the Lion of the tribe of Judah, the Root of David, has*

prevailed to open the scroll and to loose its seven seals" (Revelation 5:2-5).

No one but Christ can reveal the truths of the sealed book to us. But the book is no longer sealed! This overcoming Christ, who overcame sin and even death itself, has stepped up to open it for what Daniel called, "the time of the end."

What happened when the book was opened? For that answer we must go to the tenth chapter of Revelation:

> *I saw still another mighty angel coming down from Heaven, clothed with a cloud. And a rainbow was on his head, his face was like the sun, and his feet like pillars of fire. He had a little book open in his hand.... Then the voice which I heard from Heaven spoke to me again and said, "Go, take the little book which is open in the hand of the angel who stands on the sea and on the earth." So I went to the angel and said to him, "Give me the little book." And he said to me, "Take and eat it; and it will make your stomach bitter, but it will be as sweet as honey in your mouth." Then I took the little book out of the angel's hand and ate it, and it was as sweet as honey in my mouth. But when I had eaten it, my stomach became bitter. And he said to me, "You must prophesy again about many peoples, nations, tongues, and kings"* (Revelation 10:1-2;8-11).

At the command of the voice from Heaven, John ate the book—he didn't just look at it or read it—and it tasted as sweet as honey in his mouth. We of this season of the open book are going to have the awesome privilege of eating hidden manna, truth concealed throughout all generations until now. The implications of the fact that John ate the book are great for those of our generation.

One of the great weaknesses of the charismatic movement traditionally has been the general shallowness regarding the Word of God. It's time to wake up and get our rear in gear. As long as we are shallow in the Word, God cannot use us to the fullest dimensions that He would like to. Some of you might say, "Well, I'm a man of the Spirit!" Good for you! That's great! But you need to be a man of the Word, too! Otherwise you're nothing but dangerous! Spirit without the Word has no foundation, no anchor to keep you from grounding on the rocks of error. Others of you might say, "Well, I am a man of the Word!" All well and good, but you need to be a man of the Spirit, too. Otherwise you're deadly! The dead letter kills; it's the Spirit that gives life. What we need is a merging and marrying of the Word and the Spirit. Don't you want that? I know I do! And I believe ours is the generation that will see it—that is seeing it!

God is a restorer. He's going to restore to man everything that Adam lost. Everything that Adam forfeited because of his sin, God is going to give back—to us. Can you imagine walking in the cool of the evening like Adam once did, enjoying unbroken, unbridled, unlimited fellowship with the Lord? Get ready; it's coming!

Get Ready to Eat the Hidden Manna

God wants you to eat this hidden manna because the book is open. There is an offering of concealed truth from Heaven to be revealed only for your eyes, so that you will move in the destiny that God has for you. Matthew 13:16 says, "But blessed are your eyes for they see, and your ears for they hear." God is revealing these truths now so that you can take them and move forward in a precise way in order to get where you need to be.

Heaven is crying out to us, "No hesitation!" This is not a time for indecision but for action, to stand on the promises of

God. Paul counsels us, "Therefore, since these [great] promises are ours, beloved, let us cleanse ourselves from everything that contaminates and defiles body and spirit, and bring [our] consecration to completeness in the (reverential) fear of God" (2 Cor. 7:1 AMP). What promises? And especially, what promises are ours that would promote or inspire us to the kind of purity described in this verse? What would bring us to "cleanse ourselves from everything that contaminates and defiles body and spirit"? The answer is found in the verses just prior, at the end of chapter six:

> ...*For you are the temple of the living God. As God has said: "I will dwell in them and walk among them. I will be their God, and they shall be My people." Therefore "Come out from among them and be separate, says the Lord. Do not touch what is unclean, and I will receive you." "I will be a Father to you, and you shall be My sons and daughters, says the Lord Almighty"* (2 Corinthians 6:16-18).

God will dwell and walk among us! He will be our Father, and we will be His sons and daughters! Isn't that amazing? It's high time for us to embrace who we really are and to get down to the real business of the Kingdom of God. There are too many schizophrenic Christians torn between Christ and the world because they can't decide who they really are.

We are sons and daughters of God, which means there should be a family resemblance. John put it this way: "Beloved, now we are children of God; and it has not yet been revealed what we shall be, but we know that when He is revealed, we shall be like Him, for we shall see Him as He is. And everyone who has this hope in Him purifies himself, just as He is pure" (1 John 3:2-3). Our identity is as sons and daughters of God, and our destiny is to be like Him. This is a return to God's original plan, a restoration of His heart's desire as expressed in Genesis 1:26: "Let us make man in Our image, according to Our likeness...."

God's ultimate plan for us is that we be conformed to the image of Christ. According to Colossians 1:15, Christ is "the image of the invisible God." Invisible means what? Something you can't see. We cannot see God until we see Him in the form in which He chooses to reveal Himself. And He chose to reveal Himself as a human male, the Son of a virgin, who would bear the name Immanuel, which means, "God with us" (see Isa. 7:14; Matt. 1:23).

One day the Lord said to me, "The whole of My earthly ministry is summed up in John 17:6." So I looked it up: "I have manifested Your name to the men whom You have given Me out of the world. They were Yours, You gave them to Me, and they have kept Your Word." The key word here is *manifested*. *Invisible* means you can't see it; *manifested* means you can see it. Jesus' mission on earth was the same as ours: to make an invisible God seeable, touchable, and tangible to the world.

Job asked God, "Did You not pour me out like milk, and curdle me like cheese, clothe me with skin and flesh, and knit me together with bones and sinews?" (Job 10:10-11). What this means is that Job (and all the rest of us) went from splatter to matter, from a liquid to a solid. The same thing happened to Jesus. We, and He, took on flesh, form, and function for a divine purpose.

Jesus Christ was given a body to make an invisible God visible and known. While on earth, He lived a perfect, sinless life, took our sins upon Himself, died on a cross for our salvation, was buried in a tomb, and on the third day was raised from the dead. Forty days later, after appearing to His disciples numerous times and showing Himself alive with many infallible proofs, He ascended into Heaven, where He sits at the right hand of His Father, ever interceding for us as our great High Priest.

With Jesus gone from the earth, has God left Himself without a witness here? Absolutely not! That's where we come in! Why else would the Church be called "the Body of Christ"? We have the same mission He did, to make an invisible God known. Jesus told His disciples, "As the Father has sent Me, I also send you" (John 20:21b). As He is in Heaven, so are we in this world (see 1 John 4:17). God is going to keep on with Genesis 1:26 until it becomes a living reality. Paul said, speaking of God, "For whom He foreknew, He also predestined to be conformed to the image of His Son..." (Rom. 8:29a). One way or the other, we are going to bear His image. That's the hidden manna.

Get Ready to Receive a New Name

The second promise for over-comers in Revelation 2:17 is a white stone with a new name on it known only to the recipient. In ancient Israel, the high priest wore a pouch under his ephod that contained two stones: black for "no" and white for "yes." In Christ, the question is no longer up in the air. He has given us a white stone. That means yes! No rejection, no disqualification, but full acceptance! Full pardon! Full forgiveness! The fullness of His anointing is available to us. We have full access to God's throne of grace and full claim to the riches and resources of Heaven. We are heirs of God and joint-heirs with Christ (see Rom. 8:17). What a promise!

The name carved on that white stone is the name God gives to those who receive it. God is birthing a new thing in the earth, and only He has the right to name it. We cannot allow the movement of the past to name what God is birthing now. Let me illustrate this with a scene from the life of Jacob. "Then God said to Jacob, 'Arise, go up to Bethel and dwell there; and make an altar there to God, who appeared to you when you fled from the face of Esau your brother'" (Gen. 35:1).

Bethel, of course, is the place where Jacob had his first encounter with God. Fleeing the murderous wrath of his brother Esau, Jacob camped for the night in a place where he thought he was alone. During the night, however, he had a powerful vision of a ladder between earth and Heaven, with angels ascending and descending on it. At the top of the ladder stood the Lord, who spoke to Jacob and promised to be with him wherever he went and to bless him (see Gen. 28:10-22). Now, twenty years later, Jacob is a wealthy man with two wives, eleven sons, many servants, and large herds of livestock and flocks of sheep. God kept His word.

> *And Jacob said to his household and to all who were with him, "Put away the foreign gods that are among you, purify yourselves, and change your garments. Then let us arise and go up to Bethel; and I will make an altar there to God, who answered me in the day of my distress and has been with me in the way which I have gone." So they gave Jacob all the foreign gods which were in their hands, and the earrings which were in their ears; and Jacob hid them under the terebinth tree which was by Shechem* (Genesis 35:2-4).

Before journeying back to Bethel, Jacob made sure everyone in his household got rid of any idols or other symbols of things contrary to God's rule. Whenever we get ready to adjust our lives to God's direction and activity, the first thing we need to do is get rid of the junk of the world that we've accumulated in our lives. It gets back to this whole idea of purifying ourselves for the sake of the promises that are set aside for us. That is why it says in Hebrews, "Therefore we also, since we are surrounded by so great a cloud of witnesses, let us lay aside every weight, and the sin which so easily ensnares us, and let us run with endurance the race that is set before us, looking unto Jesus, the author and finisher of our faith" (Heb. 12:1-2a). Whenever God points out something in our lives, we need to get rid of it right away, once and for all. Otherwise, it will become a trap that will spring on us unexpectedly and bring us down.

Verse five says that Jacob and his household began their journey. Jacob was on his way back. The Church is on its way back, too. This is where the new name carved on the white stone comes in. We must be very careful or we will be in great danger of allowing the dying movement to name the coming movement.

After arriving in Bethel, Jacob did as God directed. He built an altar and worshipped the Lord there. It was at Bethel that God gave Jacob a new name: Israel. The name *Jacob* means "deceiver," while the name *Israel* means "prince of God." Jacob received a new name in keeping with his transformed character. But look what happened next:

> *Then they journeyed from Bethel. And when there was but a little distance to go to Ephrath, Rachel labored in childbirth, and she had hard labor. Now it came to pass, when she was in hard labor, that the midwife said to her, "Do not fear; you will have this son also." And so it was, as her soul was departing (for she died), that she called his name Ben-oni; but his father called him Benjamin* (Genesis 35:16-18).

During the journey from Bethel, Rachel went into hard labor. Anyone who has been active and alert in the Body of Christ over the past 15-20 years knows how the Church has been going through hard, grinding labor. Birth is at hand! The new thing that God is doing is ready to appear! Rachel died in childbirth, but she lived long enough to know that she had birthed a son and to give him the name Ben-oni, which means, "son of my sorrow."

Rachel, I believe, represents the past movement of the Church. She took it as far as she could take it, and with her dying breath she tried to place her name—lay her burden—on the fruit of her labor. But then Jacob stepped up and named the boy Benjamin, which means "the son of My right hand." In the same way, Father God is going to name the new move that He is birthing, and He is naming it, "the son of My right hand."

Aren't you tired of society trying to name you? Don't you want God to give you your new name? Something completely new is in the air, and God is bringing it into being. Everywhere I go, people ask me, "What is it going to look like?" I don't know. All I know is that it is going to be drastically different from anything that we have ever seen before. Signs and wonders and the power of God will abound in a manner unparalleled in the history of the Church. Why? Because the people of the world need to see divine power in action, evidence of the reality of a God who can change their lives forever, proof that there is a light that can lead them out of the darkness.

People are drawn by power, not by platitudes. They respond to the real deal, not to empty theories that are divorced from personal experience. We can talk about the power of God all day long, but why should anybody believe us unless they actually see His power at work in and through us and experience His power touching them in a substantive way? Every human being longs inwardly to be restored to everything Adam lost, even when they don't recognize their need or understand the source of their pain or the reason for their discontent.

So we had better get ready for signs and wonders on a dimension we've never seen before. My dear brothers and sisters, it is time for God to turn up signs and wonders because the enemy has. The devil has already turned on his light show. He is already busy dazzling and deluding people with his smoke and mirrors. Already, demonic signs and wonders are commonplace in the occultic realm and anywhere in the world where the powers of darkness hold sway. And in the meantime, the Church putters around saying, "Well I really don't know about all of that." We'd better learn! God is about to send the real fire, the real light.

The harvest is plentiful, but the workers are few (see Matt. 9:37). As the end of this present age approaches, good and evil alike will blossom. The more the Light of God expands and advances, the more the darkness will advance to try to blot it out. But it's a losing battle. John said, "In Him [Christ] was life, and the life was the light of men. And the light shines in the darkness, and the darkness did not comprehend [or overcome] it" (John 1:4-5). I've already peeked at the final pages of the story and, guess what, folks—we win!

Do you want to see God's power in your life? First of all, remember that God is sovereign; He is accountable to no one except Himself. He will manifest His power in the time, place, and manner of His choosing. Second, understand that there is no formula or equation for getting God's power in your life. There is no step-by-step plan or method.

So how do you see the power of God manifesting in your life? You have to become desperate! You have to desire His power and presence as much as or more than you desire life itself. The psalmist said, "As the deer pants for the water brooks, so pants my soul for You, O God. My soul thirsts for God, for the living God. When shall I come and appear before God" (Ps. 42:1-2). That's how desperate you must be. You must crave the presence and power of the Lord so much that you can almost taste it! Jesus described the attitude you need perfectly when He said, "Blessed are those who hunger and thirst for righteousness, for they shall be filled" (Matt. 5:6).

In addition to being desperate, you need a pure heart. Confess your sins. Get rid of all the useless junk, clutter, and emotional and spiritual baggage that you're carrying around. Ask

God to give you a clean heart and restore a steadfast spirit within you (see Ps. 51:10). Jesus said, "Blessed are the pure in heart, for they shall see God" (Matt. 5:8).

In case you need some additional promises to encourage you, try these: "For I will pour water on him who is thirsty, and floods on the dry ground; I will pour My Spirit on your descendants, and My blessing on your offspring" (Isa. 44:3). And, "The Lord will guide you continually, and satisfy your soul in drought, and strengthen your bones; you shall be like a watered garden, and like a spring of water, whose waters do not fail" (Isa. 58:11).

I believe it is up to each of us whether we have drought or a river. I don't know about you, but I want the rivers of His refreshing! I want that new name! Father God is birthing something new, and we can't let Rachel, in her hard labor, cry out in her last desperate breath, "Ben-oni, son of my sorrow!" No! Father God is speaking a new name for this new day: "Benjamin, son of My right hand!"

First John 3:2 says, "Beloved, *now* we are children of God...." I love that little word, *now*. *Now* brings us into the present. It bars the past, barricades the future, and traps us in the present. We need a move of God now! And I know that it is coming. We're headed higher than we've ever been before. Revelation 4:1 really is for us. After we open the door to Christ's knock, the King of Heaven says to us, "Come up here," and there is a door standing open in Heaven. If we go through the open door, we will find the open book. We're on an incredible journey, and it has barely begun!

CHAPTER 3

God Can Use Anyone

Have you ever felt like you were too insignificant for God to notice? One time, I was speaking in a large coliseum before several thousand people. That particular evening, the prophetic was really strong. The gift of prophecy was flowing, and God was giving people different secrets and words about themselves, and many folks were being blessed.

As I looked out across the congregation, I saw a little elderly lady sitting there, a precious lady with silver-gray hair, who looked to be in her late 70s or early 80s. The Lord said to me, "I have a prophetic word for her that will make her whole life have meaning and purpose."

I was so excited! I love giving those kinds of words to people! So I pointed her out and said, "Ma'am, would you please stand." She stood up. Then I said, "God's going to give you a word that will make your whole life have meaning and purpose." I was so excited I could barely contain myself! I asked her to stand out in the aisle. As she made her way out to the aisle, I jumped off of the platform and ran down the aisle to where she was standing, waiting. Thousands of people were closely watching everything that was happening.

Once again, I said to her, "Ma'am, God Almighty is going to give you a word that will make your whole life have meaning and purpose." What I was doing now was waiting for God to give me the word He had promised! I could hardly wait myself to hear what the Lord said to her. Finally, the Lord said to me, "Here's the word you are to give her." I said, "Okay, Lord, what is it?" He said, "Look her right in the face and say to her, 'Yes, honey, I saw you picking that duck.'"

I was absolutely devastated! What kind of a word was that? I couldn't say that to this sweet, precious, little old lady! In my spirit I protested, "No, God, I can't say that! This word is supposed to make her whole life have meaning and purpose!" But He answered, "That's what I want to tell her."

So, reluctantly and almost apologetically, I said, "Well… um…I think maybe the Lord has a word for you." Then, taking a deep breath, I looked her right in the eye, just like God had told me to do, and said, "Here is what God said to tell you: 'Yes, honey, I saw you picking that duck!'"

When I said that, the dear lady fell to the floor weeping and laughing, almost hysterical! I was stunned. "Get her up," I said. Some of the folks around her helped her to her feet. "Ma'am," I said, "what is it? What happened?"

"Oh, son," she answered, "you don't understand. When I was a young woman during the war, so many years ago, I could find no job except working for the government, standing on a dock all day, picking the feathers from the breasts of ducks to use in military clothing. One day, in the height of my desperation, I cried out, 'Oh God, do you even know where I am?'"

Now, after all those years, she was sitting in that coliseum and God had reassured her: "Yes, honey, I saw you picking that duck."

How much would the world take note of a young woman on a dock picking duck feathers? Not much. But God took note—and He remembered.

No matter how small or insignificant or unimportant you may feel sometimes, God knows who you are, and He knows where you are. He knows all about your hopes and your dreams, your fears and your disappointments. God knows everything about you and your circumstances—and He cares. Jesus said, "Are not two sparrows sold for a copper coin? And not one of them falls to the ground apart from your Father's will. But the very hairs of your head are all numbered. Do not fear therefore; you are of more value than many sparrows" (Matt. 10:29-31). God knows you through and through, down to the exact number of hairs on your head. Far from insignificant or unimportant, you are of infinite, priceless worth to God. He made you just the way you are, He loves you just the way you are, and He wants to use you—just the way you are.

Not As the World Sees

Our culture is addicted to bigness. We assume that bigger is always better. If something is good the way it is, it is bound to be even better if it's bigger. We have this crazy compulsion to "super-size" everything, not just fast-food meals. There is that annual national fixation known as the Super Bowl. There are "superstars" in Hollywood and "supermodels" on the runway. Businesses are always offering "super sales" with "super bargains." This bigness mentality has even found its way into the Church, where many believers look up to "super saints" and "mega-churches" as the ideal to strive for. In both worlds, the secular culture as well as the Church, the small and unspectacular is often pushed aside or ignored.

Not so with God. Bigger is not always better. Sometimes God reveals Himself in the most unspectacular of ways and uses the most unlikely of vessels (from the human perspective). When the prophet Elijah was waiting on the Lord, he heard Him not in whirlwind, earthquake, or fire but in a "still small voice" (see 1 Kings 19:11-12). Who would ever have imagined that a teenage boy with a sling would bring down a nine-foot-tall warrior champion with a single stone between the eyes (see 1 Sam. 17)?

God does not think the way we think or do things the way we do: "'For My thoughts are not your thoughts, nor are your ways My ways,' says the Lord. 'For as the heavens are higher than the earth, so are My ways higher than your ways, and My thoughts than your thoughts'" (Isa. 55:8-9). And since God's ways are not man's ways, He is not restricted to man's methods. God can do whatever He wants whenever He wants using whoever He wants to accomplish anything He wants. Genesis 18:14 asks the rhetorical question: "Is anything too hard for the Lord?" while Luke 1:37 trumpets the answer: "For with God nothing will be impossible."

God measures by a different standard from that of the world. This is why we who are believers must break out of the mind-set that tells us that we are little, weak, unimportant, insignificant, or useless simply because that may be the way the world sees us. The world's evaluation doesn't matter. What matters is how God sees us. The world sucks up to the rich, the famous, and the powerful. God, on the other hand, is drawn to the humble, the weak, and the unassuming (in the world's eyes). He chooses them as the instruments of His purposes. The apostle Paul explained it this way:

Where is the wise? Where is the scribe? Where is the disputer of this age? Has not God made foolish the wisdom of this world?...For you see your calling, brethren, that not many wise according to the flesh, not many mighty, not many noble, are called. But God has chosen the foolish things of the world to put to shame the wise, and God has chosen the weak things of the world to put to shame the things which are mighty; and the base things of the world and the things which are despised God has chosen, and the things which are not, to bring to nothing the things that are, that no flesh should glory in His presence (1 Corinthians 1:20,26-29).

Even the wisest wisdom of the world is foolishness compared to the wisdom of God. And next to the mind of God, the highest heights of man's intellectual achievements never even get off the ground. Yet it is the foolish, the weak, the base, and the despised of the world that God chooses to use. That certainly takes in all of us! Don't worry about God not knowing where you are. You may be in a place where you are unknown, unappreciated, and unfulfilled, but God sees you picking that duck! If God uses the foolish, weak, base, and despised of the world, He will certainly use you (and me). So just be faithful where you are, and always be available. God can and will use anyone who is willing to make himself or herself available to Him.

Why does God choose to use the discarded and disregarded of the world? So the world will see His glory. God's methods and ways always defy human logic or explanation, but they always work. A classic example is the fall of the city of Jericho to the Israelites in chapter six of the Book of Joshua. Being a walled city, and the most powerful city in Canaan, Jericho defied seizure by any natural means at the Israelites' disposal. God did not provide Joshua with the latest textbooks on military science or strategy. Instead, He gave him instructions for taking the city that were utterly unorthodox, even ridiculous, from the natural point of view.

The plan was simple: the Israelites were to march around the city once a day for six days, maintaining complete silence. Then, on the seventh day, they were to march around Jericho seven times, once again in silence. Upon completing the seventh circuit, they were to blow trumpets and shout in unison as one great voice. That was it. No battering rams, no scaling ladders, no pitched combat with sword and spear and arrow. God's plan for victory called for obedient faith, regardless of the outrageous insult to the "common sense" reasoning of the natural mind.

Of course, we know what happened. The Israelites did exactly as God commanded. On that seventh day, after finishing their seventh trip around the city, the Israelites shouted and blew their trumpets—and the massive stone walls of Jericho fell flat. The Israelites quickly took the city (see Josh. 6). All the plans and schemes of men, all the elaborate defenses and orthodox strategies proved worse than useless next to the power of God. Centuries later, God executed another unorthodox strategy when He used the "weakness" of a cross to defeat sin and death and win salvation and eternal life for all who would turn to Him in faith.

Maybe you think you are weak, with no special gifts or talents and little to offer, a "nobody" in the eyes of the world. If so, you're just the kind of person God is looking for, just the kind of person He wants to use. It is in our weakness that God shows Himself strong (see 2 Cor. 12:9). God delights in putting us in such situations so that, when all the smoke clears, He alone receives the glory. Remember, God is God. He can do anything He wants to do and is not constrained to man's choices. The Spirit of God can make a way where there seems to be no way. God knows the end from the beginning. He is Author and Finisher, not Author and Oops! Nothing catches God by surprise. He always knows just what He wants and where to find it: "For the Lord does not see as man sees; for man looks at the outward appearance, but the Lord looks at the heart" (1 Sam. 16:7b). It is when we have come to the end of ourselves that God moves in to release true power. One day the Lord spoke these extremely encouraging words to me: "Tell My people that this whole thing is My idea!" What a wonderful statement, reassuring us that God has everything under control!

Appearances Can Be Deceiving

In the call and commissioning of an instrument, God is not restricted to the choice of human judgment, which may be based upon a consideration of "apparent credentials," or the appeal to the human eye. Such was the case with the anointing of David as king of Israel. When Samuel arrived at Jesse's house to anoint one of Jesse's sons, per God's instructions, Jesse paraded his boys (all except for one) before the priest. Even Samuel was too quickly impressed by appearances:

> So it was, when they came, that he looked at Eliab and said, "Surely the Lord's anointed is before Him!" But the Lord said to Samuel, "Do not look at his appearance or at his physical stature, because I have refused him. For the Lord does not see as man sees; for man looks at the outward appearance, but the Lord looks at the heart" (1 Samuel 16:6-7).

Sometime earlier, Samuel had informed Saul, Israel's first king, that he was going to lose his kingdom because he had disobeyed God. Then Samuel said to the king, "The Lord has sought for Himself a man after His own heart, and the Lord has commanded him to be commander over His people..." (1 Sam. 13:14b). God is concerned about heart condition, not physical style and appearance. What "credentials" do you need in order to be used by God? A pure and clean heart, a heart fully surrendered to God, a heart that is after His own heart.

One by one, all seven of Jesse's sons passed in front of Samuel, and all received the same response: "He's not the one." Samuel must have been puzzled.

> *And Samuel said to Jesse, "Are all the young men here?" Then he said, "There remains yet the youngest, and there he is, keeping the sheep." And Samuel said to Jesse, "Send and bring him. For we will not sit down till he comes here." So he sent and brought him in. Now he was ruddy, with bright eyes, and good-looking. And the Lord said, "Arise, anoint him; for this is the one!" Then Samuel took the horn of oil and anointed him in the midst of his brothers; and the Spirit of the Lord came upon David from that day forward...* (1 Samuel 16:11-13).

By logical human standards, David was an unlikely choice. He was the youngest son, and he knew about shepherding, not about ruling a nation as a king. And yet, like Jesus, the Good Shepherd, any good king is always a shepherd of his people. David had what Israel needed, and God knew it. David's chief qualification was his heart full of love for God. All God needs is a willing heart; He can mold and shape the rest.

God, in His superior wisdom and knowledge, may (and often does) by-pass the most likely choice of man and reach out instead for an instrument most people would dismiss out-of-hand. In selecting the second king of Israel, God disregarded experience, rank, and seniority rights. He chose the youngest instead of the eldest, a stripling with a heart for God, in preference to a man with an attractive countenance and impressive stature. Eliab appeared to be the right choice, but he was rejected by the Lord.

Appearances may be deceiving and our own understanding inadequate. This is why Scripture admonishes us to, "Trust in the Lord with all your heart, and lean not on your own understanding; in all your ways acknowledge Him, and He shall direct your paths" (Prov. 3:5-6). We cannot rely upon the old pattern to accomplish God's new thing.

Not only is God not bound to man's methods; He also is not limited to man's means. Remember the lad who had the five loaves and two fish that Jesus used to feed 5000 people (see John 6:5-13)? The disciples, still thinking like the world, asked, "What are they among so many?" But when they were given freely to the Lord and passed under His blessing, great was the supply.

The inadequacy of man's own means, in contrast to those of God, is taught throughout the Bible. One of the God's covenant names is El Shaddai, which carries many different and powerful meanings, one of which is, "The One who will do for you what you cannot do for yourself." This is permanently written on the pages of the history of the Church and is constantly demonstrated in experience. Yet man still prefers the glitter and polish of his own machinery to the humble simplicity of God's provision. It is so easy to forget that the Lord's battles are not won by the might of numbers, nor by the power of human means, but by the Spirit of the Lord (see Zech. 4:6).

God can use the humblest person to accomplish the greatest end. The key to being used by God is remembering that, "Now we have received, not the spirit of the world, but the Spirit who is from God, that we might know the things that have been freely given to us by God" (1 Cor. 2:12). We should not be stumbling about in the dark but rather living in the light, knowing what God has promised to provide. The Lord is yet seeking those who will accept and submit to His ways. He always responds to a hungry heart. It is through people who know and willingly submit to their God that He will accomplish great exploits (see Dan. 11:32). Will you be one of them?

How Hungry Are You?

John 12:21 tells how some Greeks approached the apostle Philip and said, "Sir, we wish to see Jesus." Such also must be the deepest desire of our heart. There is today arising within the heart of God's people an immense hunger to know Him truly, not just in the head but also in active everyday life. For several years now, the Holy Spirit has been fanning the flames of discontentment, causing the people of God to become extremely hungry for Truth. All across the earth, God's people are echoing the cry of Isaiah 64:1: "Oh, that You would rend the heavens! That You would come down!" There is a growing desperation to see the mighty power of God demonstrated in our day. All across the Body of Christ, I hear the plea, "Lord, let Your works appear!" People inside and outside of the Church are tired of the polished plans of man. They long to see the raw power of God.

In a prophetic visitation, the Lord said to me, "Accept no imitations! If you will not compromise but truly stand for the truth, you can expect no limitations!" If you are truly, radically hungry, then this promise is for you. God will pour the living water of His Word and His Spirit upon you. I'm not talking about some new program at your fellowship; I am talking about a radical revolution that will transform our definition of Christianity. Remember, God never intended to establish His Kingdom with mere words but with demonstrated power (see 1 Cor. 4:20).

Let me ask you this: how hungry are you? Be honest. Are you truly desperate for God? Are you gripped with an overwhelming hunger for the reality of knowing the living God, not just in your head but deep within your heart in an imitate way? Is your heart's desire to see Jesus and be an instrument of His love, grace, mercy, and power? Are you becoming unyielding in your pursuit to move into the reality of His divine presence? He can make you hungry. He wants to make you hungry for Him. All you have to do is ask.

We are on a quest to truly know God. Now is the time to advance ever deeper into the Holy Spirit. As the Spirit of God awakens our ears to hear and opens our eyes to see, we discover that there is yet before us an expansive field of spiritual reality and that we are to venture there with the Holy Spirit to make our discoveries. Now is the time to unlock hidden treasures. Heaven is shouting, "No hesitation!" This is not a time to wait or to wander; it is a time to move confidently into the promises of God.

Just as Joshua was advised to prepare the people of Israel because they were about to go where they had never gone before, we too must prepare to go deeper. The journey to draw near is a quest that we must accept with great joy. Our present attainment of spiritual life and hunger is the result of the Lord's work in us; He alone can create that deep hunger to know Him more. It is God who is at work within us, both to will and to do His good pleasure (see Phil. 2:13). Nothing could be more important than living in such a manner as to please our Heavenly Father. In Luke 12:32, Jesus says, "Do not fear, little flock, for it is your Father's good pleasure to give you the kingdom." God takes great pleasure in children to whom He can give His Kingdom, children who are eager to receive it and manifest it in their lives. He searches the world for such people (see 2 Chron. 16:9). God is looking for mature men and women in whom He can release Kingdom power. Now is the time for action, not just talk. God longs to display His awesome power through a pure, holy, and hungry people.

Stay Hungry, Stay Humble, Press On, Move Higher

The key to continuing usefulness to God is to stay hungry and to stay humble. Every day we live should take us another step toward spiritual maturity. The Christian life is not static;

we should be continually moving from one level of spiritual understanding and experience to another. Progress will not always occur at the same rate, but we should always be moving. Our rate of progress will depend, in part, on the amount of spiritual illumination that we have obtained through our past and on our ongoing response to the Lord's presence and work within us.

An old song I've known since childhood says, "Every day with Jesus is sweeter than the day before." That should be the testimony of our lives as believers. We are either moving ahead or falling back, either growing or dying. There is no middle ground. Are you as close to the Lord as you want to be? Are you as close to Him as you used to be? Is life with Jesus sweeter for you today than it was yesterday? It is beneficial from time to time to evaluate where we stand in relation to the Lord. Drifting away is so easy to do that we can do it unawares. We need to heed the counsel of Jesus that He gave to the church at Ephesus: "I have this against you, that you have left your first love. Remember therefore from where you have fallen; repent and do the first works, or else I will come to you quickly and remove your lampstand from its place—unless you repent" (Rev. 2:4-5). Remember, repent, return; these are the keys to personal renewal and to remaining a clean and accessible vessel for the Lord's use.

The Spirit of God will guide our paths, as God disciplines and trains us in order to thrust us up into a higher realm of spiritual reality and life. Faith that is not tested is only theory. An old gospel hymn says,

> I'm pressing on the upward way,
> New heights I'm gaining every day;
> Still praying as I onward bound,
> "Lord, plant my feet on higher ground."

God has planted within the heart of His people the desire to always reach higher, never settling for less than everything that He has promised.

Your upward progress toward higher ground will be determined by the degree of your spiritual hunger, a hunger the Lord alone can create. Ask the Spirit of Truth to create within you a deeper hunger, not just for the things of God, but also for the Lord Himself. Never let your raw hunger for God dissipate. How do you stay hungry? Pray for spiritual hunger. Keep yourself immersed in the Word of God. The more living Bread you consume, the more you will want. Practice prayer regularly. Strive for a God-focused mind-set that enables you to fulfill Paul's injunction to "pray without ceasing" (see 1 Thess. 5:17). Stay connected to the Divine power source through praise and worship.

Here's another tip: never grow tired of the Truth. It is so sad to hear people say sometimes, "Oh, I know that; I've heard it before. Tell me something new." They find old truth boring; they want some new truth to tickle their ears. Where the gospel and the things of God are concerned, there is no new truth—just the old, old story kept fresh and alive and vibrant in the hearts of His children in every generation. One characteristic of children is that they love to hear their favorite stories over and over again. It should be the same with the saints. Every time we read, hear, or tell that old, old story, it should be as fresh and new for us as if it was the first time. Another old gospel hymn says,

> I love to tell the story,
> For those who know it best
> Seem hungering and thirsting
> To hear it like the rest.

How hungry are you for that "old, old story of Jesus and His love"?

How could the truth of God ever grow stale? It is so deep, we could not even begin to plumb its depths if we had a thousand lifetimes! That's why we have eternity. We will have all of forever to get to know God, going ever deeper, growing ever richer! There are thousands of facets of light in this glorious gem of redemption, which radiate from it continually. All revelation is purely a progressive seeking to make Christ Jesus known in a deeper way. The Bible is like a lovely diamond: the more light shines upon it, the more brilliance it radiates. We never see it the same way twice. It is eternally moving, and it is inexhaustible. The life of Christ within us is immense, emancipating, and liberating. Don't ever stop your quest to know Him more!

As we move into a deeper understanding of the Word of God, we must also move into a broader and a more glorious revelation of the Lord Jesus Christ. He is the Word that became flesh (see John 1:14). Jesus did not say, "I have some truth to share." Rather, He said, "I am the truth" (see John 14:6). This means that all truth is personified and has become articulate and fully expressive in Him. The closer we get to Him, the more we will love Him. All truth is summed up in this revelation from the lips of Jesus: "He who has seen Me has seen the Father..." (John 14:9b). He was not talking about seeing a physical body but rather about the manifestation of the nature and character of the Father as seen in the Son. This invisible and marvelous God the Father became visible and articulate through the physical incarnation of God the Son, eternally identified with us in the wonderful, dynamic Person known as Jesus Christ.

Those who gathered around Jesus heard Him speak and saw the manifestations of miracle power in His life. They were the recipients of His grace and healing, but not even the disciples had a revelation as to His identity. After they had followed Him for over two years, Jesus said to them, "Who am I?"

After Peter correctly identified Him as the Messiah, the Son of God, Jesus said that Peter had come to this understanding through a direct revelation from the Father, not through any observation of Jesus. Jesus then told Peter that he was hearing from the Father, just as He Himself heard (see Matt. 16:15-17). Now the disciples were ready to be lifted into a new level of revelation. He told them that He would die on the cross (see Matt. 16:21-23), and later He revealed His glory to Peter, James, and John, on the Mount of Transfiguration (see Matt. 17:1-8).

Like those disciples of old, when we begin to seek the Lord Himself, we discover that each unfolding of spiritual truth leads us to a fuller revelation and understanding of Jesus. I've been awakened to this overwhelming truth, and Jesus is becoming an increasing reality in my life. I hope the same is true for you. Our goal is to become more and more like Him.

No matter who you are, God can use you. He wants to use you, if you will let Him. He wants to anoint you and manifest His presence and power in and through you. Your part is to stay hungry, stay humble, press on, and move higher. Let your desire be like Paul's, so that you can say with him:

> *That I may know Him and the power of His resurrection and the fellowship of His sufferings, being conformed to His death; in order that I may attain to the resurrection from the dead. Not that I have already obtained it, or have already become perfect, but I press on so that I may lay hold of that for which also I was laid hold of by Christ Jesus. Brethren, I do not regard myself as having laid hold of it yet; but one thing I do: forgetting what lies behind and reaching forward to what lies ahead, I press on toward the goal for the prize of the upward call of God in Christ Jesus* (Philippians 3:10-14 NASB).

CHAPTER 4

Keep the Main Thing
the Main Thing

Even as we stay hungry, stay humble, press on, and move higher, we must be careful to keep our focus where it belongs: squarely on Jesus Christ. We must keep the main thing the main thing.

Some time ago, while ministering in Jerusalem, I was startled awake in the middle of the night by a strong, audible voice, which I believed to be the Holy Spirit, saying, "Consider Him!" Stunned, I sat straight up in bed, my entire body trembling from the holy Presence in the room. Glancing quickly at the clock, I noted that it was 4:12 A.M. I intuitively knew that this was speaking of Acts 4:12: "Nor is there salvation in any other; for there is no other name under Heaven given among men by which we must be saved."

This pre-dawn encounter with the Spirit of God convinced me totally that our highest priority must be to get to know

Christ intimately. We are truly to consider Him, the man Christ Jesus. He is the true pattern and example for our lives. In our pressing on and moving higher, we are to seek to become just like Him. The primary pursuit of our lives is Christ-likeness.

It is sad how little most of us actually know about Christ. We talk about Him all the time. We invoke His name in worship and sing His praises. We even preach His Word and proclaim Him as Savior and Lord. But do we really know Him? The only way to know a person is to spend time with that person, listening, sharing, and joining our hearts to that person's heart. Have we taken the time to listen to Jesus, to learn His heart, and to bare our hearts' desires before Him?

The New Testament constantly challenges us to take a stand regarding Christ. We cannot read the story of Jesus and remain neutral about Him. Whether from the lips of friends, foes, or Jesus Himself, the questions leap off the pages at us: "Who do men say that I am?" (Mark 8:27); "What do you think?" (regarding Jesus' claim to be the "Son of Man") (Matt. 26:66); "What then shall I do with Jesus who is called Christ?" (Matt. 27:22).

What will you do with Jesus? What have you done with Him? Have you, in your own heart and beyond all doubt, reached the same conclusion as Jesus' disciples, for whom Peter spoke when he said, "You are the Christ, the Son of the living God" (Matt. 16:16)? This is the same Jesus who promised, "I am with you always, even to the end of the age" (Matt. 28:20).

Knowing that the King of Kings and the Lord of Lords abides with us should release within us great confidence, not in our own ability but rather in His ability. Many know only "the babe of Bethlehem." Yes, without question, Christ was born in a manger in the humble city of Bethlehem of Judea (see Matt. 2:1-11). But He is more than that. Some know only the "suffering Lamb of Calvary." Again, yes, and a thousand times yes! Christ Jesus died victoriously upon the cross. But He is more than that. Jesus Christ is so much more than just a suffering, sacrificial Lamb. On the cross, Jesus was victor, not victim, crying out at the moment of His death, "It is finished" (John 19:30). Notice that He did not say, "I am finished." He was talking about the completion of His mission, not the end of His life. No one took His life from Him. He gave His life freely so that our sins could be forgiven and so that we could receiver eternal life.

Jesus came the first time as a suffering Servant who died for the sins of man. He will come a second time as Judge of all the nations, King of Kings and Lord of Lords. As His followers and intimate friends, our prayer should ever be, "Your Kingdom come. Your will be done on earth as it is in Heaven" (Matt. 6:10).

Your Kingdom Come

Jesus Christ is the most single-minded person who has ever lived. His entire earthly life, including the whole of His public ministry, was focused on one thing: announcing and establishing the Kingdom of God on earth. He announced it with His preaching, teaching, and healing; He established it through His death and resurrection. The first recorded words of Jesus deal with the Kingdom: "From that time Jesus began to preach and to say, 'Repent, for the Kingdom of Heaven is at hand'" (Matt. 4:17). When Jesus taught His disciples how to pray, the first thing He told them to ask of the Father was for His Kingdom to come to earth: "In this manner, therefore, pray: Our Father in Heaven, hallowed be Your name. Your Kingdom come. Your will be done on earth as it is in Heaven" (Matt. 6:9-10). Because the Kingdom of God was so central to the purposes and plans of Christ, He wanted His followers to constantly seek after its unveiling. If the Kingdom of Heaven was Jesus' central priority, it must be ours as well. We must keep the main thing the main thing.

The phrases "Kingdom of God" and "Kingdom of Heaven" are a common and fundamental part of biblical theology, with the word *kingdom* appearing 150 times in the New Testament alone. Its root meaning is God's royal kingship and power, His divine authority to lead and rule. God is the supreme ruler over all creation. The royal rule of Christ is invincible, imperishable, and will last forever (see Col. 1:13-20; Rev. 1:8).

Jesus declared that this gospel of the Kingdom was to be preached in all the world. Our mission on earth is to obey Him, and we need His anointing to empower us to carry out His command. As the Body of Christ, we are to live a life so yielded to Jesus that the Kingdom (the power and authority) of God is recognized here on earth, even by those who do not believe. We are to be so obedient to our King that His Kingdom will be expressed on this earth to an ever-increasing extent—no matter how much the influence of the powers of darkness grows—just as it will be shown in its fullness at the end of the age.

The Kingdom of God is more than a good method or a great message. It consists not of eloquent words, but it is a demonstration of the power of God. A well-delivered sermon or an expertly-reasoned teaching is not enough; people need to see God's power on display. The people of this generation are ready to see God's Word displayed in power and action. Only then will they begin to see and believe in the Kingdom of God and to trust Christ as their Savior and Lord. As Jesus Himself stated boldly:

> *Most assuredly, I say to you, he who believes in Me, the works that I do he will do also; and greater works than these he will do, because I go to My Father. And whatever you ask in My name, that I will do, that the*

Father may be glorified in the Son. If you ask any-
thing in My name, I will do it (John 14:12-14).

Every true believer is to be doing the works of Jesus; this is
the evidence of the Kingdom of God.

We are here on earth to do the very works of Jesus. This is
the ministry of the Kingdom. If we are to be doing the works
of Jesus, we would do well to understand what works He did.
Matthew 4:23-24 gives us a clear picture:

And Jesus went about all Galilee, teaching in their
synagogues, preaching the gospel of the kingdom, and
healing all kinds of sickness and all kinds of disease
among the people. Then His fame went throughout all
Syria; and they brought to Him all sick people who
were afflicted with various diseases and torments, and
those who were demon-possessed, epileptics, and par-
alytics; and He healed them.

We are to preach the good news of salvation, teach the
Scriptures, heal the sick, and set the captives free—just as
Jesus did.

To distract us from declaring and displaying these works,
the enemy of our souls attempts to get us to look at and live in
the past. Many believers today seem to prefer to reminisce
about the mighty moves of God in former times rather than
get involved with what He is doing now. While we should be
thankful to God for every move of the Spirit, we can't live life
always looking back. We aren't going to move forward very
fast if we're always staring in the rearview mirror. We must
see God at work in our day, today. God is the God of the NOW!
He is the great "I AM" who encompasses eternity.

Paul describes our mission and commission in terms of
government and diplomacy when he says that we are "ambassadors for Christ" (see 2 Cor. 5:20). The word *ambassador* is

the English translation of the Greek word *presbeuo*, which has the root meaning of being a senior representative possessing power and authority. An ambassador represents the government that appointed him. His power and authority are delegated. When he speaks in his official capacity as ambassador, his voice is the voice of the government he represents. In the same way we, as God's ambassadors, represent His government—His Kingdom—here on earth. He has delegated His power and authority to us for that purpose. If we are His ambassadors, we have His authority to act in His name and on His behalf. This power and authority are actively at work in us right now!

The Kingdom of Heaven is at hand! We are to declare the same message as our Master. He has entrusted His Body, the Church, with the administration and expansion of His Kingdom on earth, which He established. We must extend to the world the same invitation as Jesus when He said, "Come to Me, all you who labor and are heavy laden, and I will give you rest" (Matt. 11:28). This is an open-ended invitation, for all who will, to enter the Kingdom of Heaven. The time is now! The Kingdom of Heaven is at hand!

The Harvest is Plentiful

And while the Kingdom of Heaven is at hand, the harvest is plentiful. Jesus always kept His focus on the harvest. Regardless of the turbulent times He lived in and the temptations and potential distractions that surrounded Him, Jesus never allowed anything to derail Him from fulfilling His purpose. It is amazing to note how Jesus stayed riveted upon His life's goals. What was His secret? He knew who He was and why He was on earth, and He simply watched to see what His Father was doing and then did the same thing. Reaching and saving the lost for the Kingdom of God was always the vivid center of His focus. He said, "For the Son of man has come to seek and to save that which was lost" (Luke 19:10). He came as a King to bear witness to the truth of the Kingdom of God. In response to Pilate's question, Jesus said, "You say rightly that I am a king. For this cause I was born, and for this cause I have come into the world, that I should bear witness to the truth. Everyone who is of the truth hears My voice" (John 18:37).

The forces of the day did not determine the measure of Christ's ministry. Injustice was rampant; however, Jesus refused to settle earthly disputes (see Luke 12:13-14). Jewish nationalistic fervor was uncompromising, yet Jesus mustered no militia (see John 18:36). Thus, the ministry of Jesus Christ emerged in a world made turbulent by fierce, nationalistic zeal and false religious priorities. Even the pressure of political needs was urgent, yet Jesus did not become a politician (see John 6:15). Instead, He treated these major needs of His times as though they were incidental issues. He focused on one thing: seeking the lost and introducing them to His Kingdom.

Looking past the conflicts, issues, and horrors of His times, Jesus directed His disciples also to fix their eyes upon this most important issue. He said to them, "Lift up your eyes and look at the fields, for they are already white for harvest!" (John 4:35b). As His disciples today, we too must "lift up [our] eyes" beyond the fears and sideshows of life and see what God is looking at: "fields...already white for harvest." In a related passage, Jesus said, "The harvest truly is plentiful, but the laborers are few. Therefore pray the Lord of the harvest to send out laborers into His harvest" (Matt. 9:37b-38). All of us are called as laborers; so not only are we to pray for laborers, but we are also, as the Lord leads, to be part of the answer to our own prayers!

God is moving even now, preparing the way for an end-time harvest of massive proportions. The grace of God is powerful. Many people who always have been avowed enemies of God outwardly are, even now, inwardly being invaded by God's grace. Some of them don't even know it yet. God's desire is for all people to be saved and to come to the knowledge of the truth (see 1 Tim. 2:4). With God, not only are all things possible, but no one is impossible. Anyone is harvestable when Christ reveals Himself.

We must learn to look beyond the wars, conflicts, moral evils, and social ills of our times to focus clearly on the harvest that is ripe for the sickle. In spite of the apparent darkness of our world, the times are always right to reach the lost. Indeed, the very best thing that each of us can actually do, in light of worldwide conflict, is to win our neighbors to Christ. Many will respond because, in troubled times, people seek answers. Jesus told us to pray for the harvest and for laborers. Our role may be prayer, but our goal is evangelism. So let us be faithful, then, in prayer.

The Spirit of God is moving in every segment of society. God has already raised up people in businesses, in government, in neighborhoods, and in every nation and subculture on earth who are laborers in His harvest. Wherever God has a harvest to reap, He raises up laborers. However, because the laborers are few, they often tend to be overwhelmed and hesitant. This is why we must continually pray to the Father for laborers and then be ready to put feet to our own prayers.

There is a power that comes from God that is released uniquely from prayer, which activates the "send" signal in God's laborers. As we pray, divine appointments of God begin to take place, laborers receive supernatural opportunities, and the harvest takes on divine dimensions. This is not a time for us to be overwhelmed by the conflicts, catastrophes, and chaos in our world. Let us, even in these times of terrors and wars, be faithful in prayer to the Lord of the harvest.

If the harvest is going to come, it will have to be the work of the Lord. Bringing the harvest home is beyond our power alone. The psalmist said, "It is better to trust in the Lord than to put confidence in man. It is better to trust in the Lord than to put confidence in princes" (Ps. 118:8-9). This is His harvest; He will not allow it to rot in the fields! We must trust Him to bring it in. We must have faith that everything that God purposes to do will come to pass.

Faith Is First

True faith is fundamental to the Christian life. The writer of the book of Hebrews reminds us: "Without faith it is impossible to please Him, for he who comes to God must believe that He is, and that He is a rewarder of those who diligently seek Him (Heb. 11:6). In the arena of the supernatural manifestation of God's power, if we expected more, we would see more. Jesus said "According to your faith let it be to you" (Matt. 9:29b). If we are going to walk in a place of authority that will produce power, we must walk in faith. This level of faith is impossible unless we trust God to fulfill what He promised in Scripture.

It does not take much faith to move God, but it does require real faith. The Lord Jesus, responding to the questions of His followers about why they could not cast out a demon, answered: "Because of your unbelief; for assuredly, I say to you, if you have faith as a mustard seed, you will say to this mountain, 'Move from here to there,' and it will move; and nothing will be impossible for you" (Matt. 17:20). Mustard-seed-sized faith moving a mountain: that is real faith doing big things! And the fact that we rarely see something of that magnitude happening reveals how little or inadequate our faith really is!

The way to build your faith is to use what you have. Once I was watching world-class body builders on television and was impressed at how very well developed and sharply defined their muscles were. As I continued to watch, I sensed the Lord saying to me, "You have the same number of muscles as these men!" I was shocked. Then He continued, "But you need to develop yours." That's how it is with faith. God has given each of us a measure of faith (see Rom. 12:3), but most of us need to spend more time building it up and developing it.

Faith increases when we hear and heed the Word of God. A good foundation of the Word of God is essential if we are to have strong faith. The Word of God is a Rock on which to build our lives. As an old gospel hymn puts it,

> On Christ the solid Rock I stand,
> All other ground is sinking sand.

How true! If our lives are not founded on the clear teachings of the Word of God, we are not on a firm foundation. The first big storm of life to come along will wash us away.

Our reward will be great if we will place our confidence and trust in the living God. Note this wonderful promise found in Jeremiah:

> *Blessed is the man who trusts in the Lord, and whose hope is the Lord. For he shall be like a tree planted by the waters, which spreads out its roots by the river, and will not fear when heat comes; but its leaf will be green, and will not be anxious in the year of drought, nor will cease from yielding fruit* (Jeremiah 17:7-8).

In this verse, we discover the promise of fruitfulness and refreshing as we walk in confident trust with the Lord.

The promise of protection and provision comes when we trust the Lord with all our heart:

Trust in the Lord with all your heart, and lean not on your own understanding. In all your ways acknowledge Him, and He shall direct your paths. Do not be wise in your own eyes; fear the Lord and depart from evil. It will be health to your flesh, and strength to your bones. Honor the Lord with your possessions, and with the first fruits of all your increase; so your barns will be filled with plenty, and your vats will overflow with new wine (Proverbs 3:5-10).

Trusting the Covenant-Keeper

We can trust God because the Bible reveals Him to be a covenant-making, covenant-keeping God. The Bible itself is a covenantal book, being divided into two sections, the Old and New Testaments (Covenants). These covenants comprise the plans and purposes of God. But what exactly is a covenant?

In modern society, the word *covenant* has lost some of the fullness and richness that it had in Bible times. Covenant deals with the promise to fulfill what has been spoken and pledged. We can be certain that what God has promised, He will fulfill. Not one promise will fall to the ground. We can trust God to keep His word. God has promised to keep us in perfect peace if we will fully trust Him. In these uncertain times, this is the place of safety, where we cast all our cares upon the Lord, knowing that He cares for us. It is time to draw near to God with our hearts full of faith, knowing that He is watching over His own. Trust will produce confidence and lasting peace: "You will keep Him in perfect peace, whose mind is stayed on You, because he trusts in You. Trust in the Lord forever, for in YAH, the Lord, is everlasting strength" (Isa. 26:3-4).

Proverbs 18:10 says, "The name of the Lord is a strong tower. The righteous run to it and are safe," and David the psalmist writes, "Those who know Your name will put their trust in You; for You, Lord, have not forsaken those who seek You" (Ps. 9:10). In the revealed names of God, we can discover much concerning His promises, as well as His provision for His people.

When God spoke to Moses and said His name was the Lord God, it also meant that He was a God who was active on behalf of His people. God's personal name, Yahweh, translated most often as Lord, means, "I will be what I will be." It declares the activity of God. His name shows that He will be all that is necessary to His covenant people as their needs arise.

The name of God signifies the active presence of God, the covenant-maker and covenant-keeper, on behalf of His own. He is not just a God who exists as a being for Himself; He is also a God who is active in covenantal power to supply all that His people will ever have need of.

Scripture tells us clearly that God is our only true place of protection. When our trust rests wholly upon Him, He will be our fortress and our refuge: "The Lord is my rock and my fortress and my deliverer; my God, my strength, in whom I will trust; my shield and the horn of my salvation, my stronghold. I will call upon the Lord, who is worthy to be praised; so shall I be saved from my enemies" (Ps. 18:2-3). Now is the time to sow these precious promises into your heart and soul. Commit these words to memory; they will be beacons of bright hope in dark days.

In a timely message for these days, the prophet Haggai states: "'Be strong, all you people of the land,' says the Lord, 'and work; for I am with you,' says the Lord of Hosts" (Hag. 2:4b). During these dark days, as we war against wicked, demonized hearts, may we stand strong in this testimony: "In God I have put my trust; I will not be afraid. What can man do to me?" (Ps. 56:11).

Are You a Disciple?

Knowing that our God is a faithful, covenant-keeping God strengthens our faith, and a strong faith is a prerequisite for following Jesus as a true disciple. When Jesus called His first disciples, Simon Peter and his brother Andrew, He said simply, "Follow Me, and I will make you fishers of men" (Matt. 4:19b). He calls all of us today to the same occupation. The Lord Jesus is beckoning us as His beloved Bride to fully follow Him. He has extended the invitation; have you responded? It is time to lay down our plans and follow the Lord.

Truly following Jesus requires a total commitment of our lives and wills to Him. Jesus laid out the requirements very clearly: "If anyone desires to come after Me, let him deny himself, and take up his cross, and follow Me. For whoever desires to save his life will lose it, but whoever loses his life for My sake will find it" (Matt. 16:24b-25). In a related passage, He says, "If anyone serves Me, let him follow Me; and where I am, there My servant will be also. If anyone serves Me, him My Father will honor" (John 12:26).

During these days of preparation, nothing is more crucial than you being with Jesus and His presence being with you. This was Moses' desperate cry to God—that His presence would be with His people: "If Your Presence does not go with us, do not bring us up from here. For how then will it be known that Your people and I have found grace in Your sight, except You go with us?" (Exod. 33:15b-16a). God delights in those who desire Him. It is from those who seek after Him that He chooses His disciples.

It is easy to understand why God chose Joshua to be Moses' successor as the leader of Israel. The key is found in Exodus 33:11: "So the Lord spoke to Moses face to face, as a man speaks to his friend. And he would return to the camp, but his servant Joshua the son of Nun, a young man, did not depart from the tabernacle." Joshua loved being in the presence of God. Those who pursue the presence of God will find themselves following Christ and being formed into His disciples.

Jesus' call to His disciples was to follow Him. But what exactly is a disciple? The New Testament word for *disciple* is *mathetes*, which means, "a learner." It comes from the root word *manthano*, which means, "to learn." This word deals with doing, not just hearing. A disciple is one who has a belief that is accompanied by behavior inspired and driven by that belief. Our beliefs change our attitudes, which in turn change our actions. We can say we believe something, but until what we believe changes our behavior, we are just living in deception. So the word *disciple* denotes "one who actively follows another's teaching."

Note that a disciple is not only a student but also a follower. As such, disciples imitate their teacher. Too many would-be disciples in our day are looking to classes instead of picking up their crosses. If we settle for becoming students without pressing on to become followers, we are in grave danger of becoming dead in spirit and bound in legalism. On the other hand, if we try to be followers without first becoming true students, we run the high risk of ending up as superficial, shallow, cotton-candy Christians with no power or influence to affect the world for Christ.

A total commitment is crucial if we are to fulfill of the Great Commission. In the Christian walk, we are about to find out that well done is better than well said. Remember, the Kingdom of God is both Word and power. Revival came in Samaria when the people heard and saw the miracles Philip was performing: "And the multitudes with one accord heeded the things spoken by Philip, hearing and seeing the miracles which he did" (Acts 8:6). In the very first verse of the Book of Acts, Luke, the author, refers to his earlier writing, his Gospel, as "The former account I made...of all that

Jesus began both to *do and teach*" (Acts 1:1). Disciples involve themselves in both Word and action; anything else is self-deception: "But be doers of the word, and not hearers only, deceiving yourselves" (James 1:22).

By these criteria, are you a disciple?

Marks of a Disciple

It has been said, "We cannot direct the wind; however, we can adjust the sails." The time has come for the Church to turn her sails to catch the wind of discipleship. We do not have time to waste; our only preparation for tomorrow is the right use of today. Scripture declares, "Behold, now is the accepted time; behold, now is the day of salvation" (2 Cor. 6:2b). It is time for all of us as believers to stop arguing and debating about what a Christian is—and to start living like one! We need to press on beyond simple belief to become active, obedient, following disciples of Christ.

As never before in history, we have today an open door to reach out with the gospel of the Kingdom of God to touch hurting humanity. The Great Commission is not a suggestion! It is a command! We need to lay aside our differences and work together to share the good news with those who need to hear it. The apostle Paul spoke about the importance of sound doctrine, but he also said that if on some points we disagree, we should not let that divide us. Instead, he exhorted us to keep walking out what we know while allowing God to make clear any apparent contradictions: "Therefore let us, as many as are mature, have this mind; and if in anything you think otherwise, God will reveal even this to you. Nevertheless, to the degree that we have already attained, let us walk by the same rule, let us be of the same mind (Phil. 3:15-16).

There is no need to wonder whether or not we are disciples of Christ. Jesus clearly defined what His disciples would look like. First of all, disciples are abiders: "If you abide in My word, you are My disciples indeed" (John 8:31b). When we abide in Christ's Word, we confirm that we are His disciples. We must be like trees planted by the deep rivers of God's Word in order to bring forth fruit that will remain.

Second, disciples of Christ are doers. Their understanding of the Word, gained from their abiding, will bring positive and practical action. They will be like prized apple trees in September, bearing much fruit for the Kingdom: "By this My Father is glorified, that you bear much fruit; so you will be My disciples" (John 15:8). Remember, Jesus is looking for doers, those who will be fruit-filled and fruitful.

Third, and most important of all, disciples of Christ are lovers. The greatest proof of our discipleship will never be our dogmatic adherence to some doctrine or the great deeds we do in Jesus' name, but rather our love one for another: "By this all will know that you are My disciples, if you have love for one another" (John 13:35). Our love for each other is, in fact, the only proof we have to show the world that God is real and the gospel is true. Let us choose to abide in His Word, press on to fruitfulness, and walk in His love so that the world will know that we are Christ's disciples—and many will turn to Him. That is why Jesus came, and it is why we are here. Bringing the lost into the Kingdom of God is the main thing.

And we must keep the main thing the main thing!

CHAPTER 5

Who Shall Ascend?

Personal discipleship is a central element to keeping the main thing the main thing. And a key to discipleship is to keep growing. Never satisfied with the status quo, true disciples are always seeking to learn more, to press in deeper and to rise higher. Their eyes are always on Jesus, as their hearts sing,

> I'm pressing on the upward way,
> New heights I'm gaining every day,
> Still praying as I onward bound,
> "Lord, plant my feet on higher ground."

They identify fully with Paul's words: "Forgetting those things which are behind and reaching forward to those things which are ahead, I press toward the goal for the prize of the upward call of God in Christ Jesus" (Phil. 3:13b-14). They are blessed because they "hunger and thirst for righteousness" and trust the Lord to fill them (see Matt. 5:6). Like the Jewish pilgrims of old, who yearly made the upward trek to Jerusalem for the Passover, disciples of Christ always seek to ascend the hill of the Lord.

If King David was alive today, he would be a disciple of Christ because he always had a heart for God. David understood the principles of discipleship. He knew that following the Lord was an upward journey. This is why, in Psalm 24:3, David poses two very pertinent questions: "Who may ascend into the hill of the Lord? Or who may stand in His holy place?"

The Jerusalem of David's day, a small city built on top of a hill called Mt. Zion, is but one section of the much larger city of today, but it is still known as "the city of David." In the Bible, however, the phrase, "hill of the Lord" always refers to the place of God's anointing, the place of His Power. So David's twin questions carry a double meaning. More than simply asking about those making a pilgrimage to the city, David wants to know who will ascend to receive the anointing of the Lord. Who will stand in His holy place as vessels of His presence and His supernatural power?

David answers his own questions in the next verse: "He who has clean hands and a pure heart, who has not lifted up his soul to an idol, nor sworn deceitfully" (Ps. 24:4). Those who ascend stand to gain a great reward: "He shall receive blessing from the Lord, and righteousness from the God of his salvation" (Ps. 24:5).

All of us should aspire to ascend into the hill of the Lord. Our hearts' desire should be to enter into the very presence of God, to come into the place where He can anoint us, bless us, and equip us to be a blessing to others. Who shall ascend into the hill of the Lord? Those who have clean hands and a pure heart. *Hands* speak of action, while *heart* speaks of attitude, and if we want to ascend the hill of the Lord, we must deal with both.

Attitude Determines Altitude

Actions reflect attitude. Regardless of what we say, our attitudes will manifest in our actions. I'm not speaking so much about our mental attitudes, or how we feel at any given moment, but our heart attitudes, our innermost natures, the natural inclination of our wills either toward or away from God. We can put on a masquerade and fool people for awhile, but eventually our true natures will come out. That which is inside us will manifest on the outside, and it is what is inside that matters. The fruit reveals the root. Jesus made this clear when he stated:

> *For a good tree does not bear bad fruit, nor does a bad tree bear good fruit. For every tree is known by its own fruit. For men do not gather figs from thorns, nor do they gather grapes from a bramble bush. A good man out of the good treasure of his heart brings forth good; and an evil man out of the evil treasure of his heart brings forth evil. For out of the abundance of the heart his mouth speaks* (Luke 6:43-45).

And in another place, He said:

> *What comes out of a man, that defiles a man. For from within, out of the heart of men, proceed evil thoughts, adulteries, fornications, murders, thefts, covetousness, wickedness, deceit, lewdness, an evil eye, blasphemy, pride, foolishness. All these evil things come from within and defile a man* (Mark 7:20-23).

We must be very careful to guard our hearts because out of the heart springs the issues of life (see Prov. 4:23). God says in Jeremiah, "The heart is deceitful above all things, and desperately wicked; who can know it? I, the Lord, search the heart, I test the mind, even to give every man according to his ways, according to the fruit of his doings" (Jer. 17:9-10). The Lord knows our hearts. He knows how "deceitful" and "desperately wicked" they are. Do you see your heart that way? Do I? This is a truth none of us likes to face. But the same Lord who knows how deceitful and wicked our hearts are also searches our hearts and tests our minds and can transform both—if we let Him.

Our attitude determines our altitude. If our desire is to be faithful disciples and to ascend the hill of the Lord, we should learn to pray daily in a spirit of openness similar to David's when he said, "Search me, O God, and know my heart; try me, and know my anxieties; and see if there is any wicked way in me, and lead me in the way everlasting" (Ps. 139:23-24). It is always easy to perceive (and point out) other people's faults and flaws but much harder to be honest about our own. We must give the Lord permission to search our hearts and reveal to us what He finds there. When God puts his finger on any "wicked way" in us, what are we supposed to do with it? Confess it to Him quickly! Scripture says, "He who covers his sins will not prosper, but whoever confesses and forsakes them will have mercy (Prov. 28:13). That's what we must do if we are going to ascend into the hill of the Lord.

To confess means to agree; we agree with God concerning our sin. When we confess our sin to the Lord genuinely, honestly, open-heartedly, and in a spirit of humble repentance, "He is faithful and just to forgive us our sins and to cleanse us from all unrighteousness" (1 John 1:9). Then, according to Psalm 103:12, He removes them from us as far as the east is from the west. When God forgives our sins, He remembers them no more (see Jer. 31:34). He forgets them entirely, which means that He will never bring them up again to shame us or to hold them over us. They are drowned and gone forever in a sea of forgetfulness.

It's one thing to ascend into the hill of the Lord but quite another thing to abide there. We ascend by having clean hands and a pure heart—right behavior resulting from a right heart attitude. But what does it mean to abide? How do we do it? Once again, we turn to Scripture for the answer, and to David, who was an expert in ascending and abiding:

> *Lord, who may abide in Your tabernacle? Who may dwell in Your holy hill? He who walks uprightly, and works righteousness, and speaks the truth in his heart; he who does not backbite with his tongue, nor does evil to his neighbor, nor does he take up a reproach against his friend; in whose eyes a vile person is despised, but he honors those who fear the Lord; he who swears to his own hurt and does not change; he who does not put out his money at usury, nor does he take a bribe against the innocent. He who does these things shall never be moved* (Psalm 15:1-5).

Those with clean hands and a pure heart may ascend into the hill of the Lord, but abiding is for those who walk uprightly, work righteousness, and speak truth in their hearts. In a way, Psalm 15 is a commentary, a practical description of what it means to have clean hands and a pure heart. This psalm describes the character qualities that will manifest in our lives when we make clean hands and pure hearts our ongoing lifestyle. Upright behavior, righteous deeds, truthful speech that never backbites, kindness toward all, hatred of evil, fear of the Lord, refusal to be greedy, and moral uprightness with a strong sense of justice—these are the qualities of the people of God who may abide in His holy hill, the people who are positioned to receive His anointing.

Psalm 91:1 says, "He who dwells in the secret place of the Most High shall abide under the shadow of the Almighty." Isn't that where you want to be? I know I do. We have to learn to dwell in the secret place of the Most High. We have to learn to abide under the shadow of the Almighty. We have to learn to dwell in His holy hill. Learning to abide in the

Lord's presence is very, very important. It is one of the most critical keys to receiving and walking in His anointing. God is not satisfied with only infrequent visits from us, and we should not be satisfied either. He longs for us to tarry in His presence. We like spending time with people we love. How much time do you spend seeking and tarrying in the presence of the Lord? To what altitude will your attitude take you?

What Do You Do When You Have Failed?

It's good to aspire to ascend into the hill of the Lord and to abide in His presence. That should be the chief desire of every Christian. But what if you've messed up along the way? What if you have made such a mess of your life and feel you have gotten so far away from the will of God that you wonder if you can ever return? Is there any hope for you? Can God still use you? Is there a way back from the pit of discouragement and failure?

Yes! There is always a way back. And David shows us the way. David was a man after God's own heart who knew the secrets to ascending the hill of the Lord and abiding there. But he was also a highly flawed human being (as we all are) who messed up big time, yet he made his way back into the grace and favor of God. Whenever I look at the experience of David, I am encouraged because I know there is hope for me! And I want you to know that no matter where you are or what has happened in your life, there is hope for you too!

David loved God with all his heart and sought to serve and honor Him all the time, yet he fell into sin that quickly escalated into disaster and led to repercussions and consequences that followed him for the rest of his life. It all started one fine spring evening when David took a walk on the roof of his palace.

It happened in the spring of the year, at the time when kings go out to battle, that David sent Joab and his servants with him, and all Israel; and they destroyed the people of Ammon and besieged Rabbah. But David remained at Jerusalem. Then it happened one evening that David arose from his bed and walked on the roof of the king's house. And from the roof he saw a woman bathing, and the woman was very beautiful to behold. So David sent and inquired about the woman. And someone said, "Is this not Bathsheba, the daughter of Eliam, the wife of Uriah the Hittite?" Then David sent messengers, and took her; and she came to him, and he lay with her, for she was cleansed from her impurity; and she returned to her house. And the woman conceived; so she sent and told David, and said, "I am with child" (2 Samuel 11:1-5).

It was the time of year when kings led their armies in battle, but David stayed in Jerusalem, while Joab led Israel's armies. That was David's first mistake—he was not where he should have been. A mistake in judgment took David out of alignment with God's will, and that mistake set him up for a fall. Getting out of God's will always leads to discontentment. While walking on his rooftop, David happened to see a beautiful woman bathing nearby. And he looked at her. Now, there's looking and then there's LOOKING! Upon seeing her, David could simply have said, "Oh!" but he said "Ahhhhh!" and lust was born in his heart.

One thing quickly led to another. Upon inquiry, David learned that her name was Bathsheba and that she was the wife of Uriah, one of his mightiest and most loyal warriors. That did not stop David, however, who was in the grip of lust. He sent for Bathsheba and she came. Who could resist a summons from the king? David had sex with her and she became pregnant.

Anxious to cover up this awkward situation, David ordered Uriah home from the battlefront, got him drunk, and told him to go home to his wife. That way, David hoped, when the baby came, Uriah would assume it was his. As Scottish author and novelist Sir Walter Scott wrote,

> Oh what a tangled web we weave,
> When first we practice to deceive!

Unfortunately, Uriah didn't play along. He was too disciplined and loyal a soldier to allow himself the pleasures of home and wife while his comrades were still in the field. Instead, he slept at the king's palace.

When this ploy failed, David became desperate. He sent Uriah back to the field with sealed orders to Joab to put Uriah in the thick of the fighting and then withdraw from him so he would be killed in battle. This time the king's plan worked. Uriah died and David was free to marry Bathsheba, which he did. In one of the classic understatements of all time, the Bible ends its account of this sordid affair with the words: "But the thing that David had done displeased the Lord" (2 Sam. 11:27b).

David, a man after God's own heart, was now an adulterer and a murderer. He had transgressed the laws of both God and man. How could this have happened? How had David ended up on such a sinful, immoral path? Even more importantly, was there a way back?

Confession and Repentance: The Road Back

The worst thing that can happen to an anointed person, or to any child of God, for that matter, is for them to get away with their sin. Sin corrupts. Sin destroys. Sin separates us from the favor and fellowship of God. Fortunately, God won't let us get away with sin. He always confronts us in a way intended to draw us back to Him. This is just what He did with David.

God sent a bold prophet named Nathan to confront the king with his sin. Nathan did this by appealing to David's strong innate sense of justice and righteousness. He told the story of a rich man who, unwilling to take from his own abundant flocks to prepare a meal for a houseguest, took the single ewe lamb that belonged to a poor neighbor and prepared it instead, depriving the poor neighbor and his family of a beloved pet. David was outraged, declaring that the callous, unfeeling rich man deserved to die and must make four-fold restitution. Nathan then looked David straight in the eye and said, "You are the man!"

The truth of Nathan's words shocked David awake to the reality and magnitude of what he had done. His immediate response was to humble himself in confession and repentance (see 2 Sam. 12:1-15). This is the only appropriate response when faced with the reality of our sins. God forgave David, but temporal consequences still followed in the wake of his sinful behavior. First of all, the child born of that adulterous affair died soon after birth (see 2 Sam. 12:18). And for the rest of his life, David's reign was filled with violence, war, and unrest; and rebellion, division, sexual immorality, and murder came from within his own family. David's very sins that he tried so hard to cover up visited him later in very large and very public ways.

None of this minimizes the sincerity and genuineness of David's repentance, however. Our sin often sets in motion consequences that not even confession and forgiveness will alter. David, nevertheless, confessed his sin to God in a true spirit of repentance and received God's forgiveness. As a result of his experience, David penned one of the most moving of all the psalms and one that expresses beautifully the heart and spirit of true confession and repentance. Psalm 51 is unlike any other psalm in the Bible. Where every other psalm is highly poetic, with melodious language that flows like a river, Psalm 51 is written in a ragged, "ejaculatory" style, as if spoken in spurts of deep, crushing grief and sorrow. This is only fitting since this psalm arose out of the deepest sobs of David's thoroughly broken and contrite heart. And out of the depth of David's emotions, we can see laid bare the process for abiding in the Lord. Psalm 51 illustrates how to get our lives right with God after a fall.

Look how he begins:

> *Have mercy upon me, O God, according to Your lovingkindness; according to the multitude of Your tender mercies, blot out my transgressions. Wash me thoroughly from my iniquity, and cleanse me from my sin* (Psalm 51:1-2).

No excuses, no evasion, no hem-hawing, no beating around the bush. David knew he was guilty. He also knew he had nothing to stand on except the mercy of God. Like David, we all always stand in need of God's mercy. David speaks of the "multitude" of God's "tender mercies." Lamentations 3:23 says that God's mercies are "new every morning." The God of more than enough always has mercy to lavish on us when we ask.

David's honest and straightforward confession continues in the next couple of verses:

> *For I acknowledge my transgressions, and my sin is always before me. Against You, You only, have I sinned, and done this evil in Your sight—that You may be found just when You speak, and blameless when You judge* (Psalm 51:3-4).

Never is there even a hint from David that Bathsheba may bear any of the blame at all. It was his lust, his desire, and as king, he was in a position to have his way. As far as David was concerned, the responsibility was his alone. In true confession, there is no room for passing the buck, for spreading the blame around in an effort to mitigate our own guilt. We must accept full responsibility for our actions and, as David did, recognize that God is the offended party whenever we sin. Other people may suffer, as Bathsheba and Uriah did, but the offense against God is even greater.

David refers to three different degrees or levels of sin that he needs to be cleansed of: transgression, iniquity, and sin. Transgressions are accidental sins, the sins we stumble into sometimes when we are not careful to guard our steps. We don't mean to sin, but we do it anyway because of our own weakness. Iniquity refers to unknown sins, sins we commit out of ignorance because we don't know any better. We cross the line somewhere because we don't know where the line is. Because of their accidental or unintentional nature, transgressions and iniquity receive lighter judgment. By far, the most serious of the three is sin, which in this context refers to deliberate, premeditated disobedience. You know exactly where the line is and you say, "I don't care; I'm going to cross it anyway." First Samuel 15:23 makes the sin of rebellion equal to the sin of witchcraft. Because it involves willful rebellion, this level of sin receives the harshest judgment from God. David obviously felt that he was guilty of all three, and he wanted to be thoroughly cleansed of all three.

Likewise, we need to know that our sins—at whatever level—are blotted out and cleansed. Every one of them was covered at Calvary. Christ took all of our sins upon Himself. Whenever confession and repentance are in order, we can be confident of receiving complete cleansing because Christ has already washed us in His blood.

Hyssop and Broken Bones

As if he wants to make sure he is absolutely clear on his desire for cleansing, David gets very graphic and specific:

> *Purge me with hyssop, and I shall be clean; wash me, and I shall be whiter than snow. Make me hear joy and gladness, that the bones You have broken may rejoice* (Psalm 51:7-8).

The word purge means to eradicate or flush out. It refers to a harsh but complete and thorough cleansing that leaves no traces of impurity behind. Hyssop is an extremely abrasive weed that was used for scouring. Lepers, in fact, often used hyssop to scrape away the rotted flesh from their bodies in order to prevent gangrene and prolong their lives. They would scrape away the old flesh all the way down to new flesh. So when David prayed, "Purge me with hyssop," he was saying, "Deal radically with my sin. Flush it out and eradicate it. Scour it away completely!"

David then asked to "hear joy and gladness, that the bones You have broken may rejoice." What bones? This is an analogy drawn from David's years as a shepherd. All shepherds carried a staff, a thick wooden rod about eight feet long with a curve in it, which they used for direction and protection. The staff itself provided defense against predators as well as a means of guiding the sheep in the direction the shepherd wanted them to go. The crook at the end of the shaft served to extract or draw back a wayward sheep that had gotten separated from the flock.

The worst place for a sheep is outside the flock. Lacking any natural defenses, a lone sheep is helpless against predators. Occasionally a sheep would come along that had a rebellious streak and simply would not stay with the flock. The shepherd would retrieve it and put it back with the others. Sometimes, however, a particularly stubborn and rebellious sheep would call for more drastic measures. In those instances, the shepherd would lay his staff across his knee, pick up the rebellious little lamb and break one of its legs over the staff. Then he would bind the broken leg, put the lamb in his shepherd's bag, which resembled a papoose, and carry the lamb close to him until its leg healed. After that experience, that little lamb would always stay closer to the shepherd than any of the others.

David was acknowledging that he had been like a rebellious lamb that had strayed from the flock, requiring his Shepherd, the Lord, to "break" him in order to bring him back into the fold. In like manner, the Lord will discipline us when we go astray. Like the breaking of a bone, His discipline may be painful, but He will do whatever He has to do to get our attention and bring us back to Him before we suffer even greater pain. The Book of Hebrews says that the Lord disciplines His children out of love and because they are His children, just as an earthly father disciplines the children he loves (see Heb. 12:7-11). Discipline from the Lord is proof that we are His sons and daughters.

A Clean Heart and a Steadfast Spirit

Now that he had been disciplined and had his eyes opened, and now that he had grieved over and confessed and repented of his sins, David wanted to hear joy and gladness. He wanted to know that everything was all right again. He wanted to return to the joy of open fellowship with God and to his regular practice of praise, worship, and upright living. Accordingly, he prayed:

Create in me a clean heart, O God, and renew a steadfast spirit within me. Do not cast me away from Your presence, and do not take Your Holy Spirit from me. Restore to me the joy of Your salvation, and uphold me by Your generous Spirit. Then I will teach transgressors Your ways, and sinners shall be con-verted to You. Deliver me from the guilt of bloodshed, O God, the God of my salvation, and my tongue shall sing aloud of Your righteousness. O Lord, open my lips, and my mouth shall show forth Your praise. For You do not desire sacrifice, or else I would give it; You do not delight in burnt offering. The sacrifices of God are a broken spirit, a broken and a contrite heart—these, O God, You will not despise (Psalm 51:10-17).

What do we need in order to ascend into the hill of the Lord and abide in His presence? Clean hands and a pure heart. A clean heart, a heart that cries out, "Oh God, my desire is to walk in your will at all costs. Whatever it takes, let me walk with You and abide in Your presence!" Whenever sin intrudes, the pure heart prays, "Please, Lord, put your finger on it." And when He does, the pure heart prays, "Lord, please extract this from me!" The Lord always answers the prayer of confession and repentance. Then, afterward, we can rejoice with David, in words that he very well may have written out of his joy at being restored following his sins regarding Bathsheba and Uriah:

Blessed is he whose transgression is forgiven, whose sin is covered. Blessed is the man to whom the Lord does not impute iniquity, and in whose spirit there is no deceit (Psalm 32:1-2).

These are the ones who may ascend into the hill of the Lord. These are the ones who may abide in His presence. These are the ones who are ready to receive His anointing!

CHAPTER 6

God Has Anointed You

God releases His anointing on His children for one main purpose: to bring the lost to Himself. Some time ago, I spoke at a church in Frederick, Maryland, which is near Washington, DC, and after the service the pastor and his wife took me to dinner. It was one of those fancy restaurants that required advance reservations and employed several nicely dressed young women as hostesses to seat the customers: a really first-class dining establishment. As one of these young hostesses led us to our table, the Lord said to me, "I want to win her to me."

I could already sense somehow that this young woman was very cold and hostile towards the gospel, so I said to God, "Lord, I don't think she's ready to hear much right now."

"But I am ready to win her to Me," He replied.

I knew better than to argue with the Lord, but all through the meal I kept wondering how God was going to reach this hostile woman and bring her to Himself. As we got ready to leave, the pastor paid the check, and we started out through the same door by which we had entered. Once again the Lord spoke to me: "I still want to win her."

"How, Lord?" I asked.

He replied, "Ask her about the spider web tattoo around her belly button with the black widow spider crawling towards it."

I have to admit that I felt a little awkward. The pastor and wife who were my hosts were elegant, dignified people who probably were not very familiar with tattoos and such or with this kind of workings of the Lord, and I was afraid the whole situation would be an embarrassment to them and perhaps to me as well. Nevertheless, I called them over to me and shared what the Lord had said He wanted to do, hoping to prepare them for it. When I said that the Lord wanted to win that young woman to Him, the pastor said, "Oh, delightful!" But as I told them about the spider web tattoo, he said, "Really!" and his wife's eyes got big and round. Then he asked, "What are we going to do?"

I said, "We're going to go over there and ask her about it." What else could we do? The Lord had made His will clear; we could either obey or not. So we walked over to the same hostess who had seated us earlier, and I said to her, "I just wanted to tell you that Jesus Christ is the Son of God and He loves you dearly." Her eyes just sort of glazed over as if she was trying to tune me out. I took a deep breath and pressed on. "He's going to do something for you that'll show you just how much He loves you. God has a plan for your life. He just showed me something about you, and the only reason He did it was because he wants so much for you to be saved." She eyed me warily. Then I said to her, "I don't know you. We've never met before, have we?"

"No," she replied, "we've never met."

"Let me ask you a question. Do you have a tattoo of a spider web with a black widow crawling towards your belly button?"

Her eyes grew wide, her mouth fell open, and she screamed, "I can't believe this!" Then she flipped up the bottom of her shirt and, sure enough, there was the web and spider tattoo. She was completely disarmed. All her defenses and hostility evaporated, and she began crying. This God who knew all about her also knew she was ready to open her heart. The pastor and his wife then led her to Christ right there! Some months later, I made a return visit to that church, and guess who I saw sitting there in that sanctuary? That's right. The girl with the tattoo. Isn't God amazing?

I love it when God reveals those kinds of things about people. Why does He do it? Because He is after their hearts. He wants to draw them out of spiritual darkness into the light of His eternal love. Peter tells us that the Lord is "not willing that any should perish but that all should come to repentance" (2 Pet. 3:9b). Likewise, Paul says that God "desires all men to be saved and to come to the knowledge of the truth" (1 Tim. 2:4).

This doesn't mean that everyone will be saved. God's desire is for everyone to be saved, but no one will be saved unless they hear and respond to the gospel message. That's where we come in as believers. Paul said:

> *For "whoever calls on the name of the Lord shall be saved." How then shall they call on Him in whom they have not believed? And how shall they believe in Him of whom they have not heard? And how shall they hear without a preacher? And how shall they preach unless they are sent?.... So then faith comes by hearing, and hearing by the word of God* (Romans 10:13-15,17).

We are called as ambassadors for Christ and ministers of reconciliation to share the gospel with lost people so that they can have the opportunity to be saved (see 2 Cor. 5:18-20). The Lord gives us His anointing to empower us and enable us to carry out His "great commission" to make disciples of all the nations (see Matt. 28:18-20). Early in His public ministry, Jesus said, regarding His mission from His Father:

> *The Spirit of the Lord is upon Me, because He has anointed Me to preach the gospel to the poor; He has sent Me to heal the brokenhearted, to proclaim liberty to the captives and recovery of sight to the blind, to set at liberty those who are oppressed; to proclaim the acceptable year of the Lord"* (Luke 4:18-19).

As believers and disciples of Christ, we have His Spirit dwelling inside us, and because of this, we have the same mission He did. We also have His anointing. If Jesus needed the anointing of his Father in order to carry out His mission, how much more do we need it!

We Need the Anointing

The Lord never requires anything of us that He does not equip us to do. And to fulfill our mission and commission as believers, we need His anointing. Why? Because we can do nothing without it. Actually, Jesus said, "Without Me you can do nothing" (John 15:5b), but because the anointing is so inseparably attached to Christ, the meaning is the same. The anointing represents the indwelling presence and power of the Lord, without which we truly can do nothing of lasting significance or value in the Kingdom of God. It doesn't matter how gifted we are, how talented we are, how athletic we are, or how intelligent or well educated we are. Without Him we can do nothing.

"Without Me you can do nothing." The first time I read that, I felt insulted. Then I thought, "Well, maybe I don't understand what He means by nothing." So I looked up the Greek word for nothing and really got blown away. In Greek, the word for nothing (oudeis), means, well—nothing. Nada. Zilch. Absolute zero with a vacuum in the middle of it. As a matter of fact, if any word can mean "less than nothing," oudeis is that word. Jesus was saying, in other words, that apart from Him, apart from His divine touch on all that we say and do, our lives will accomplish absolutely, totally nothing.

But lest we become discouraged over this, we need to remember that as believers we have Christ Himself living in us through His Holy Spirit. And the Christ who said, "Without Me you can do nothing," is the same Christ through whom we can do all things as He strengthens us (see Phil. 4:13). By ourselves we can do nothing, but with His anointing we can change the world!

This is why, if we want to walk in the anointing of God, we must become completely dependent upon the Holy Spirit. We were created for fellowship with God, to walk with Him and partner with Him in exercising dominion over the created order. The happiest people I know are those who are walking under the canopy of God. I have never met people more content than those who are walking under the destiny of God for their lives. We need the anointing because without it we cannot fulfill our full destiny in Christ.

We need the anointing because we have been commissioned to do the works of Christ. Jesus said, "Most assuredly, I say to you, he who believes in Me, the works that I do he will do also; and greater works than these he will do, because I go to My Father" (John 14:12). Our Lord has commissioned us to do a wonderful task, but He doesn't expect us to do it without His touch. In fact, it would be unjust and unfair of Him to give us an assignment without an anointing.

Many Christians, unfortunately, either out of ignorance or out of eagerness to be about the Lord's work, rush out without seeking or waiting for His anointing, and then they wonder why they see few results. That's not the Lord's way. He will never set us about the task He has given us without first placing that touch of Heaven on our lives. And more often than not, receiving that touch is a matter of waiting on Him.

We need the anointing of the Lord, and any one of us who wants it can receive it. I've said it many times before, and I'll say it again because many Christians still have trouble really, truly believing it: the anointing is not for Christian "superstars"; it is for every believer. In reality, there are no Christian "superstars." There may be some self-righteous "fat cats" who think they are God's greatest gift to the Church, but God thinks differently. Anyone who is full of himself or herself has no room for the anointing. The only "superstar" is the One who made the stars, the Word who was in the beginning, who was with God and who was God (see John 1:1). This is why God loves to use the humble and the broken; for they are the ones who have no illusions about themselves; they know they are nothing without Him.

The Bible tells us that, on the Day of Pentecost, the Holy Spirit came down and filled all who were in that upper room (see Acts 2:4). Not just the apostles and not just the men, but everyone in the room was filled with the Holy Spirit. Everyone in that room poured out onto the streets of Jerusalem, speaking in other tongues and boldly proclaiming the gospel of Christ. And there we find a critical key. The Spirit of God gives us the anointing not so that we can get a chill down our spine but so that we can proclaim the Word of God with boldness and power.

The Anointing: What Difference Does It Make?

Does the anointing really make that big a difference? Just ask the seven sons of Sceva:

> *Now God worked unusual miracles by the hands of Paul, so that even handkerchiefs or aprons were brought from his body to the sick, and the diseases left them and the evil spirits went out of them. Then some of the itinerant Jewish exorcists took it upon themselves to call the name of the Lord Jesus over those who had evil spirits, saying, "We exorcise you by the Jesus whom Paul preaches." Also there were seven sons of Sceva, a Jewish chief priest, who did so. And the evil spirit answered and said, "Jesus I know, and Paul I know; but who are you?" Then the man in whom the evil spirit was leaped on them, overpowered them, and prevailed against them, so that they fled out of that house naked and wounded. This became known both to all Jews and Greeks dwelling in Ephesus; and fear fell on them all, and the name of the Lord Jesus was magnified* (Acts 19:11-17).

Sceva's seven boys thought that all they needed to cast out demons was to invoke the name of "Jesus whom Paul preaches." They didn't even preach in the name of Jesus themselves, yet they thought they could appropriate His power. They found out differently when the demonized man they were trying to deliver overpowered them and "tanned their hides!" There is no such thing as second-hand anointing.

Does the anointing really make a difference? Just ask Simon Peter. The big, rough, and impetuous fisherman was a man of great courage whose heart was in the right place but whose impulsiveness sometimes affected his judgment. Like that night in the Garden of Gethsemane, when Peter single-handedly took on a whole mob of soldiers and temple police sent to arrest Jesus, attacking them with a single dikara, an 18-inch-long short sword. Had Jesus not stopped him, there would have been a lot more blood shed than just the severed ear of Malchus, the high priest's slave (see John 18:1-12).

Yet just a few hours later, during Jesus' trial, "fearless" Peter was left quaking in his sandals when a servant girl in the high priest's household accused him of being one of Jesus' men. He denied it. In fact, over the course of maybe two hours, Peter denied Jesus three times, each time more vehemently than before. The third time, he even threw in a couple of curses and swear words to be even more convincing (see Matt. 26:69-75; Mark 14:66-72; Luke 22:54-62; John 18:15-27). Obviously, courage alone was not enough.

Fast-forward about 53 days to the Day of Pentecost. Peter, one of the 120 newly Spirit-filled believers who streamed out of that upper room, stood up and boldly and publicly preached Christ in a powerful sermon that brought 3000 new believers into the Kingdom of God. From then on, and for the rest of his life, Peter was steadfast, not only in courage, but also in spiritual power.

What changed? What happened in Peter's heart? Acts 1:8 happened. Just before He ascended into Heaven, Jesus promised His disciples: "You shall receive power when the Holy Spirit has come upon you; and you shall be witnesses to Me in Jerusalem, and in all Judea and Samaria, and to the end of the earth" (Acts 1:8). Ten days later, that promise was fulfilled at Pentecost. What happened to change Peter's life? The anointing happened. The anointing transformed Simon Peter from a guy who couldn't stay stuck to a man who preached the boldest, most powerful sermon in history. And 3000 souls are in Heaven today because of it.

The Power of the Anointing

The anointing took away Peter's instability. It took away his fear of man. It firmly anchored his faith and thoroughly grounded his love for Christ. When Peter spoke to the crowd of onlookers in Jerusalem that day, he pulled no punches:

> *Men of Israel, hear these words: Jesus of Nazareth, a Man attested by God to you by miracles, wonders, and signs which God did through Him in your midst, as you yourselves also know—Him, being delivered by the determined purpose and foreknowledge of God, you have taken by lawless hands, have crucified, and put to death; whom God raised up, having loosed the pains of death, because it was not possible that He should be held by it.... Therefore let all the house of Israel know assuredly that God has made this Jesus, whom you crucified, both Lord and Christ* (Acts 2:22-24,36).

Are these the words of a man who is trying to impress people because he is afraid of what they will think of him? No. He's under the anointing now. He's not afraid to stand up. He's not afraid to speak out. He's not afraid of what men can do to him. His only concern is to bear faithful witness to his Lord. We too need the anointing that rested on Peter to rest on us so that our tongues will be loosed, as his was, and so that we will stand up and boldly bear witness in both word and action, just as he did.

Many of us today do not speak boldly because we are afraid of offending people or turning them away. Lost people need to be confronted with the truth in a straightforward but compassionate manner. Peter certainly did not coddle his listeners. He told them what they needed to hear and his words had a powerful effect:

Now when they heard this, they were cut to the heart, and said to Peter and the rest of the apostles, "Men and brethren, what shall we do?" Then Peter said to them, "Repent, and let every one of you be baptized in the name of Jesus Christ for the remission of sins; and you shall receive the gift of the Holy Spirit. For the promise is to you and to your children, and to all who are afar off, as many as the Lord our God will call." And with many other words he testified and exhorted them, saying, "Be saved from this perverse generation." Then those who gladly received his word were baptized; and that day about three thousand souls were added to them (Acts 2:37-41).

Peter's listeners were "cut to the heart" under the conviction of the Holy Spirit. The Greek word for cut, *katanusso*, means to "pierce thoroughly," to "agitate violently," and to "prick." It means they were slashed to the very center of their souls. Does that sound "seeker friendly"? Not to our modern ears. But in reality, it is seeker friendly because seekers need to hear a gospel that will slash them to the very center of their souls so that they will be moved to repent of their sins and trust Christ. Part of the problem with much of the Church today is that we have drifted far away from preaching a gospel that makes people conform to it. Instead, we mold and conform the gospel we preach to appeal to and appease the minds and hearts of wicked men. That's why we so desperately need the anointing. The anointing will bring us back to the heart of the gospel. The anointing will bring lost people face to face with a God who they can no longer ignore, who they must make a decision about.

The power of the anointing is found not in what we "do" but in holy living, since we are confident that Christ has already "done" all the work for us. His work of redemption on the cross is a finished work. All we have to do is step into Him and invite Him to step into us. Paul said, "For to me, to live is Christ, and to die is gain" (Phil. 1:21). We let Christ live His life through us. It is a yielded life, a surrendered life, a life free from the fear or worry of having to "do enough" to please God and earn His favor. As His beloved and anointed children by faith, we already have His favor.

Paul tells us in Ephesians:

> *For by grace you have been saved through faith, and that not of yourselves; it is the gift of God, not of works, lest anyone should boast. For we are His workmanship, created in Christ Jesus for good works, which God prepared beforehand that we should walk in them* (Ephesians 2:8-10).

See, it's not about what we have done but what He has done. Our part is to place our lives completely and totally in His hands, saying, "Here I am, Lord! Anoint me! Live your life through me." And He will. He will take what we yield to Him. That's what the anointing is all about.

The Anointing is Available to Every Believer

Any believer can receive the anointing. Any believer. God plays no favorites. The ground is level at the foot of the cross. Every believer, without exception, comes to Christ through repentance of sin and faith in the One who covered their sins with His blood. And without exception, every believer has the same access to the presence and power of the Lord. The difference between those believers who receive and walk in the anointing and those who do not is, as we have already seen, a matter of hunger. Those who receive the anointing are those individuals who are hungry enough to pursue it.

Hunger is the critical key, but motivation is important also. Why do you want the anointing? Do you want it for yourself, for your own personal enjoyment or benefit, or do you want it so you can help others? Are you after your own glory, or do you seek to glorify God? When Jesus spoke the words recorded in Luke 4:18-19, which we looked at earlier, He was in the synagogue in His hometown of Nazareth, reading from the prophet Isaiah. Putting those words into their larger context reveals the purpose of the anointing both for Jesus and for us:

> *The Spirit of the Lord God is upon Me, because the Lord has anointed Me to preach good tidings to the poor; He has sent Me to heal the brokenhearted, to proclaim liberty to the captives, and the opening of the prison to those who are bound; to proclaim the acceptable year of the Lord, and the day of vengeance of our God; to comfort all who mourn, to console those who mourn in Zion, to give them beauty for ashes, the oil of joy for mourning, the garment of praise for the spirit of heaviness; that they may be called trees of righteousness, the planting of the Lord, that **He may be glorified*** (Isaiah 61:1-3).

"That He may be glorified"—that is the reason for the anointing. When God is glorified, people turn to Him. When Christ is lifted up, people are saved. As Jesus Himself said, "And I, if I am lifted up from the earth, will draw all peoples to Myself" (John 12:32). When the gospel of Christ is preached in the power of the anointing, lives are changed and destinies are altered forever. Dead religion is supplanted by vibrant, living relationship with the living God. Every eye is focused on the Lord. If your heart's desire is to glorify the Lord, to exalt His name before men and see the lost come to Christ, then your heart is in the right posture to receive and walk in the anointing.

Jesus' mission on earth was to preach the good news, heal the brokenhearted, liberate those in spiritual bondage, and comfort the mourning, replacing their sorrow with joy. As His friends and followers, we have the same mission. Maybe you are thinking, "But I'm not a preacher," or "I'm not a counselor." That's okay. Can you be a friend? Many people today pass each day in crushing loneliness. They need a friend, someone who will care about them and take a genuine interest in them as people with hopes and dreams, joys and sorrows. Being a friend does not require any special training. All it takes is a sensitive and compassionate heart. Who can you be a friend to today? Who can you encourage with a kind or comforting word? Who can you pray for or with? Opportunities to bless others and to glorify Christ are all around you. All you have to do is look.

Ordinary People, Extraordinary Anointing

Many Christians assume that the anointing normally manifests in extraordinary ways and situations. In reality, the anointing usually operates best in the most ordinary of circumstances.

One day, Peter and John were on their way to the temple when they saw a man crippled from birth sitting by the temple gate called Beautiful begging for alms. Nothing extraordinary in that: beggars were common in Jerusalem, and this man had begged at this same gate every day for years. It was a day like any other, except for the anointing of the Lord, which was about to touch this man and change his life forever. When he saw Peter and John about to enter the temple, he asked for alms.

And fixing his eyes on him, with John, Peter said, "Look at us." So he gave them his attention, expecting to receive something from them. Then Peter said, "Silver and gold I do not have, but what I do have I give you: In the name of Jesus Christ of Nazareth, rise up and walk." And he took him by the right hand and lifted him up, and immediately his feet and ankle bones received strength. So he, leaping up, stood and walked and entered the temple with them—walking, leaping, and praising God. And all the people saw him walking and praising God. Then they knew that it was he who sat begging alms at the Beautiful Gate of the temple; and they were filled with wonder and amazement at what had happened to him (Acts 3:4-10).

Peter and John probably did not go to the temple with the deliberate intention of healing a crippled beggar, but in the daily course of life, they saw a need and addressed it. That's how the anointing works best, with no fanfare and in response to needs and opportunities that cross our paths. It is also the way Jesus operated. He steadfastly refused to produce signs or miracles on demand but always responded to a simple, humble cry for help.

The healing of the crippled beggar occurred with no fanfare, but the result certainly drew a crowd. Walking unassisted on his own two feet for the first time in his life, the beggar entered the temple with Peter and John, "walking, leaping, and praising God." It was the ninth hour, the hour of prayer at the temple. Imagine how his joyous entrance must have broken up the prayer service! A crowd quickly gathered. Seeing his opportunity, Peter flowed with the anointing:

Now as the lame man who was healed held on to Peter and John, all the people ran together to them in the porch which is called Solomon's, greatly amazed. So when Peter saw it, he responded to the people: "Men of Israel, why do you marvel at this? Or why look so intently at us, as though by our own power or godliness we had made this man walk? The God of Abraham, Isaac, and Jacob, the God of our fathers, glorified His Servant Jesus, whom you delivered up and denied in the presence of Pilate, when he was determined to let Him go. But you denied the Holy One and the Just, and asked for a murderer to be granted to you, and killed the Prince of life, whom God raised from the dead, of which we are witnesses. And His name, through faith in His name, has made this man strong, whom you see and know. Yes, the faith which comes through Him has given him this perfect soundness in the presence of you all" (Acts 3:11-16).

Peter and John were ordinary men—fishermen—who had been touched by God in an extraordinary way to do extraordinary deeds for His glory. They were ordinary men who walked in an extraordinary anointing. And they were quick to give credit where credit was due. Peter used this occasion of the healing of a crippled beggar to give glory to God and to proclaim Christ to those in the temple, some of whom, at least, had clamored for Jesus' death not many weeks before.

God likes to anoint ordinary people because He knows they won't try to take the glory for themselves. In the power and flow of the anointing, we will always direct the gaze of others to the Lord. The moment we try to point to ourselves, we step out of God's will and shut ourselves off from the flow. Always, always, always we must point to Christ. He is our joy, our strength, our destiny. And He is the hope of the nations.

The Spirit of the Lord is upon us. God has anointed us— you and me—for these very days that we are living in. No previous generation has had the opportunity that we have to impact the world with the gospel of Jesus Christ. He has called, commissioned, and anointed us to do His works—and even greater works—in the earth so that multitudes will be drawn to Him. God has anointed you. What will you do?

CHAPTER 7

Receiving the Anointing

Only those who are truly hungry and thirsty for the things of God will receive the anointing, because they are the only ones desperate enough to pursue it. That's how I received the anointing. I was so desperate for "something more" that it brought me to a crisis point in my ministry. Let me tell you about it.

I remember standing before our church family in First Baptist Church of Bullard, Texas, and saying, "If this is all there is to the ministry, I am through with it." I was sick and tired of hearing people say the days of miracles were passed, that Jesus no longer healed and delivered. I could no longer explain away such verses as Mark 16:17-18, "And these signs will follow those who believe: In My name they will cast out demons...they will lay hands on the sick, and they will recover."

You see, I am a realist. I feel we must do what the Bible teaches. We are to be "doers of the word, and not hearers only" (James 1:22). I became very dissatisfied with the emptiness and lack of power that I was experiencing in my life and seeing in the lives of all the pastors I knew. I had not experienced the anointing Jesus said I could and should have as a believer.

I became hungry and desperate for more of God. "As the deer pants for the water brooks, so pants my soul for You, O God. My soul thirsts for God, for the living God. When shall I come and appear before God?" (Ps. 42:1-2). I found myself like David when he cried out, "O God, You are my God; early will I seek You; my soul thirsts for You; my flesh longs for You in a dry and thirsty land where there is no water. So I have looked for You in the sanctuary, to see Your power and Your glory" (Ps. 63:1-2). I began to cry out for God to fill this hunger, and I became desperate for the power of God to be demonstrated in my life for His glory.

The Lord then began to speak to me and give me promises—such as Isaiah 43:19-21:

> *Behold, I will do a new thing, now it shall spring forth; shall you not know it? I will even make a road in the wilderness and rivers in the desert.... I give waters in the wilderness and rivers in the desert, to give to My people, My chosen. This people I have formed for Myself; they shall declare My praise.*

God said He would open up for me rivers in the desert. Well, I was sure in a desert—a place that is dry and barren. Yet God is so very, very faithful and merciful. He will never forsake those who are truly hungry and thirsty. "For I will pour water on him who is thirsty, and floods on the dry ground; I will pour My Spirit on your descendants, and My blessing on your offspring; they will spring up among the grass like willows by the watercourses" (Isa. 44:3-4).

I began to pray and seek God. I could not go on without the power that Jesus had promised me in His Word. "Behold, I give you the authority to trample on serpents and scorpions, and over all the power of the enemy, and nothing shall by any means hurt you" (Luke 10:19). The Holy Spirit continually brought this Scripture before me. I was sick of the world mocking and scoffing the Church of Jesus Christ, saying, "Where is your God?"

One Sunday in October, 1989, I had an extremely busy and trying schedule. My day was as full as it could get. I was scheduled to preach twice on Sunday morning, then go to Rock Hill Baptist Church, thirty miles away, and preach a funeral service at 2:00 p.m., then come back to First Baptist Church in Bullard for our 25th wedding anniversary reception at 3:30 p.m., and then preach two more times that night. As I was returning from the funeral service, the Holy Spirit spoke to my heart and said, "As your day is, so will your strength be." I wasn't sure exactly what He meant, but I said, "It sounds good to me!"

In the service that evening, my wife Carolyn was sitting next to me before I was to preach. I knew she was very tired and exhausted from all of her hard work and the hectic schedule she had been keeping, so I just placed my hand on the back of her neck and was softly praying for God to give her strength. She took my hand away and said, "Bobby, your hand is so very warm. It is like an electric heating pad on my back." Then she said, "I feel great. Do you think you should offer to pray for anyone else who might need refreshing and healing?" So I invited people to come forward who wanted prayer, and as I lifted my hand to pray for them, the power and presence of the Holy Spirit overcame them, and many simply fell over under God's power. When they got up, they were refreshed and some were healed. This was one of the first times that God demonstrated His power in my life.

A few months later, Benny Hinn was coming to a nearby church. God told me that if I would go and have him lay hands upon me, I would receive the same anointing that is upon his life. At that time, I didn't know anything about Benny Hinn or the mighty miracle ministry that God had given to him. After Benny Hinn had ministered, he sat down on the platform, and as another person stood to speak, God said, "Bobby, I want you to get up out of your seat and walk up to Brother Benny Hinn and tell him what I have told you about his laying hands upon you so you will receive the anointing upon your life that I've placed upon him." So I did.

Not one person tried to stop me. Men parted in front of me like the Red Sea parted in front of Moses. I came to Benny Hinn and explained to him why I had come. He looked intently into my eyes and said, "Put your hand on the back of my neck." He prayed for me and laid his hands upon me, and the Holy Spirit placed an anointing upon my life. I will never be the same. God is opening great doors of opportunity for Carolyn and me to go all over the United States and other countries to carry our Demonstrations of God's Power Miracle Crusades.

God wants to anoint all of us. He desires to raise up many little, unknown, insignificant nobodies, like Bobby Conner, to shake nations so that Jesus Christ will get the glory. It is not our wisdom, strength, or position that will make the world take notice, but it is the anointing of God.

> *For you see your calling, brethren, that not many wise according to the flesh, not many mighty, not many noble, are called. But God has chosen the foolish things of the world to put to shame the wise, and God has chosen the weak things of the world to put to shame the things which are mighty; and the base things of the world and the things which are despised God has chosen, and the things which are not,*

to bring to nothing the things that are, that no flesh should glory in His presence (1 Corinthians 1:26-29).

Be very sure, there will be no superstars in this great move of God's Spirit—only Jesus will get the glory and the honor.

If you are hungry and humble, God will anoint you. Ask God to place a real hunger for His holiness and for His anointing in your heart. If you get desperate and thirsty enough, you will receive a fresh anointing.[1]

Fresh Oil

I've always liked fast cars. When I surrendered to preach, my pastor had a '68 GTO. It had a 441 cubic inch engine with two factory-installed four-barrel carburetors and a hydro-stick. At the time, it was the fastest car you could buy off the showroom floor. Man, I loved that car!

Today, if I wanted a fast car, I might go to the Chevrolet dealer and check out the Corvette or, even better, the Dodge dealership to drool over the Viper. If I'm really dreaming, I'd peruse the Ferraris and the Lamborghinis. All of these sports cars have powerful, precision-balanced, fine-tuned engines that provide performance plus! Let's say I lease or (since we're dreaming!) buy one. It has almost no miles on it, has a full gas tank, has been oiled and lubricated, and is ready to go. I jump in and—vroom!—off I go!

That car might run for a year or even two years, but if I never changed the oil, even that high-performance engine would eventually grind to a halt. It doesn't matter what's under the hood if you don't pay attention to what's in the crankcase. Without fresh oil, even the top-performing car in the world will burn out and be left sitting by the side of the road.

In the same way, there are many Christians who burn out and drop out because they don't know how to maintain fresh oil. I don't care how gifted you are—what you have "under the hood"—you have to learn how to walk daily under a fresh anointing if you want to keep your gifting fresh. The Holy Spirit imparts gifts to us, but we have to maintain the anointing. It is not automatic. Just as yesterday's movements of the Spirit will not suffice for what God wants to do today, yesterday's anointing will not equip us for the Kingdom work that lies before us today.

Jesus taught us to pray, "Give us *this day* our daily bread" (Matt. 6:11). The Israelites in the wilderness gathered every morning only the manna needed for that day because God renewed it every day. In the same way, the Holy Spirit renews our anointing on a daily basis—if we let Him. Just as we should not expect or desire to live on yesterday's stale and moldy bread, neither should we expect or desire to function today under yesterday's anointing. Like a high-performance car, we too need fresh oil regularly.

But like I said above and several other times so far in this book, if you want to receive the anointing, you have to be hungry for it. You have to have a real, deep, desperate, yearning hunger and thirst for the anointing, or you'll never see it. Mild interest or a lukewarm attitude simply won't do. Why should God entrust His anointing to you if you feel as though you can take it or leave it? I did not receive the anointing until I became so tired of things as they were and so desperate for something more that I was ready to pursue it at all costs. If you're stranded in the desert, the one thing on your mind is finding water to quench your thirst. Nothing else matters because your survival is at stake. It's the same way with the anointing. If you reach the place where you are ready to do anything or to part with anything in order to get the anointing, that's when you are ready to receive it. God satisfies the hungry and the thirsty.

We have to let God fan the hunger in our hearts. I feel so sad for people who are satisfied with the status quo. Let's be honest now, are you truly satisfied with the way things are right now in the Church as a whole? Are you satisfied with the level of God's presence and power that you are seeing in your own church? In your own life? Wouldn't you like to see more miracles, more healings, more lost people coming to Christ? If so, then seek fresh oil! Seek it for yourself and for others in your church. Seek it so that the Lord will be glorified in your midst more and more!

Calling the Zadok Priesthood

I believe that in the days in which we are now living, God is calling the Zadok priesthood to stand before His people:

> *"But the priests, the Levites, the sons of Zadok, who kept charge of My sanctuary when the children of Israel went astray from Me, they shall come near Me to minister to Me; and they shall stand before Me to offer to Me the fat and the blood," says the Lord God. "They shall enter My sanctuary, and they shall come near My table to minister to Me, and they shall keep My charge.... And they shall teach My people the difference between the holy and the unholy, and cause them to discern between the unclean and the clean* (Ezekiel 44:15-16,23).

It is a sad state of affairs when even the people of God don't know the difference between the holy and the unholy or the clean and the unclean. Another word for *unholy* is *profane*. I was shocked when I asked the Lord for His definition of *profane*. He said, "The profane is anything man is doing that I did not initiate. It is everything that is empty and worthless and without any eternal value." We must take particular care to make sure that what we're doing is to advance the Kingdom of God and not for our own agendas.

Jesus Christ was the supreme example of this when He said in the Book of John that He did only what He saw His Father doing and said only what He heard His Father say (see John 5:19; 8:26). That's the secret to maximizing ministry. Don't say anything until you hear what He says. Don't do anything until you see what He is doing.

The real tragedy in the Church today is that we can do things without the Lord's touch and nobody knows the difference. Billy Graham once said that if the Holy Spirit was extracted from the Body of Christ today, few people inside or outside the Church would ever notice any change. For far too long, we have been having church without God, and I believe He's tired of it. I believe He's going to start visiting our churches in a big way, and when He comes, things will be vastly different.

Jesus Christ walked in the anointing, and everywhere He went people gathered in droves to see Him, to hear Him, to touch Him. Mark records a typical occurrence: "And again He entered Capernaum after some days, and it was heard that He was in the house. Immediately many gathered together, so that there was no longer room to receive them, not even near the door. And He preached the word to them" (Mark 2:1-2). Wouldn't it be something if that verse described your church and mine on a weekly basis?

But so many of our churches today have shut Jesus out, often without even being aware of it. And now He stands outside, knocking to be let back in, as with the church in Laodicea: "Behold, I stand at the door and knock. If anyone hears My voice and opens the door, I will come in to him and dine with him, and he with Me" (Rev. 3:20). This is why so many Christians don't understand the difference between the holy and the unholy and why so many have lifestyles that are virtually indistinguishable from those of people in the world. Whenever we shut Christ out of our lives and our churches, both lose their distinctiveness. Why should the world flock to the Church if they cannot see that we have anything to offer that they cannot get somewhere else? We need the anointing to restore our distinctiveness in the world.

The Cost for the Anointing? Everything.

Power always comes at a price. In life, there is no such thing as a "free lunch." Something must be given up to gain something else. Sacrifice in the short term is necessary for advantage in the long term. People in business and every other area of life are always asking, "What's the bottom line?" Before committing to anything, they want to know, "How much will this cost?"

Counting the cost is a wise move, as long as it doesn't become the sole criterion for our decision or lead us to become cynical. Jesus Himself encouraged us to count the cost of discipleship before committing ourselves to follow Him:

> *Whoever does not bear his cross and come after Me cannot be My disciple. For which of you, intending to build a tower, does not sit down first and count the cost, whether he has enough to finish it—lest, after he has laid the foundation, and is not able to finish, all who see it begin to mock him, saying, "This man began to build and was not able to finish"* (Luke 14:27-30).

So what will it cost to get the anointing? Everything you have. Not every believer is a serious disciple of Christ, because not every believer chooses to walk in the Spirit. And those who do not walk in the Spirit will not walk in the anointing. Therefore, discipleship and the anointing go hand in hand. Just three verses later, Jesus says, "So likewise, whoever of you does not forsake all that he has cannot be my disciple" (Luke 14:33).

Don't make the mistake of interpreting this solely in financial or material terms. Following Christ and walking in the anointing may indeed require at times the giving up of some personal conveniences, possessions, or material comforts, but to "forsake all" goes deeper than the material world alone. Jesus is talking here about a heart attitude of holding nothing in this world closer or dearer to us than we hold Him. Everything that we are and have is secondary to following Christ and doing His will. Only such a total sell-out to Jesus qualifies us to carry His anointing. It is in this sense that receiving the anointing will cost you everything.

It will cost you in the area of suffering. Jesus said that no servant is greater than his master (see John 13:16). How did the world as a whole treat Jesus when He walked in perfect power and perfect love? They hated Him. They spit on Him, beat Him, lashed His back down to the bone, pulled His beard out, nailed Him to a cross naked, and then ridiculed Him as He hung there bleeding and humiliated. If that is the treatment the Master received, what can His servants expect?

The only reason most of us are not suffering or undergoing persecution very much is because we are not walking with Him as closely as we should be. If we want to experience the power of Christ working in us, we need to be willing to experience His suffering as well. Being true disciples of Christ and walking in His anointing means that we must identify with Him in every way, the positive as well as the negative, the pleasant as well as the unpleasant. Paul described the ideal disciple's attitude when he wrote:

> *But what things were gain to me, these I have counted loss for Christ. Yet indeed I also count all things loss for the excellence of the knowledge of Christ Jesus my Lord, for whom I have suffered the loss of all things, and count them as rubbish, that I may gain Christ and be found in Him, not having my*

own righteousness, which is from the law, but that which is through faith in Christ, the righteousness which is from God by faith; that I may know Him and the power of His resurrection, and the fellowship of His sufferings, being conformed to His death, if, by any means, I may attain to the resurrection from the dead. Not that I have already attained, or am already perfected; but I press on, that I may lay hold of that for which Christ Jesus has also laid hold of me. Brethren, I do not count myself to have appre-hended; but one thing I do, forgetting those things which are behind and reaching forward to those things which are ahead, I press toward the goal for the prize of the upward call of God in Christ Jesus (Philippians 3:7-14).

Carrying the anointing will, at times, cost you in terms of convenience, time, dignity, reputation, respectability, and per-secution. But in the midst of all of these things will come great advancement in the Kingdom of God. And in light of that, all the inconvenience and suffering will fade into in-significance.

Consider the experience of Paul and Silas in Acts chapter 16. Arrested, beaten, and chained to the wall of a prison in Philippi, Paul and Silas could easily have been morose and despondent. Instead, they were heard at midnight, singing and worshiping and praising God! What happened? You re-member the story. God rocked the prison with an earthquake, and the shackles fell off of every prisoner in the place! Yet not a single one escaped (see Acts 16:25-34). There is just some-thing magnetic about people anointed by the Holy Spirit who stay true to God, even in the most adverse of circumstances. Not only did all the other inmates stick around to be near Paul and Silas and their message, but also the warden of the prison and his entire family came to Christ that night. No matter the situation, the anointing of the Lord can empower and enable us to present a faithful and winsome witness that can lead to lives being forever changed in Christ. Are you hungry for that kind of spiritual power and the influence to see people's lives changed?

How Do You Get the Anointing?

I hope that by now you are so hungry for the anointing that you can almost taste it! I hope you are squirming in your chair saying, "Okay, Bobby, okay! You've convinced me! I need the anointing, and I want the anointing! Now how do I get it?"

Remember, there is no "magic formula" for the anointing, and it is not reserved for an elite group of Christian "superstars." Any Christian who is hungry enough to make the necessary preparations of heart, mind, will, and spirit can receive the anointing.

Let's talk about four "steps" for receiving the anointing. The first two will be a review because we've already talked about them in this book. They are so important, however, and so indispensable, that they bear repeating.

First, become discontent with your dry, dead, empty form of religion, and get desperate for a fresh move of God in your life. We must have a deep hunger and longing for more of the presence of God. We must cry out for God like a man in the desert cries out for water. "I stretch forth my hands unto thee: my soul thirsteth after thee, as a thirsty land" (Ps. 143:6 KJV). When we get desperate and begin to seek for the Lord with all of our hearts, then He will be found. God is looking for someone who is longing for His anointing. God wants to pour His Spirit out upon us like a flood.

Yes, if you are longing for the Lord, deeply desiring Him, and truly seeking Him, you are on the right road to receiving the anointing. "Then you will call upon Me and go and pray to Me, and I will listen to you. And you will seek Me and find Me, when you search for Me with all your heart" (Jer. 29:12-13).[2] Are you hungry? Are you desperate? Do you thirst after the Lord and His anointing like a parched land thirsts for water? I hope so. That's the first step.

The second step to receiving the anointing is to be clean and pure. Ecclesiastes 9:8 says, "Let your garments be always white; and let your head lack no oil." To be vessels that the Lord would delight to use, we must be clean. Ask God to have the Holy Spirit search your heart and convict you of any hidden or known sin.

After the Holy Spirit has searched your heart and convicted you of sin, sincerely confess your sins and repent. "If we confess our sins, He is faithful and just to forgive us our sins and to cleanse us from all unrighteousness" (1 John 1:9). Put your sins under the precious cleansing blood of Jesus. "Though your sins are like scarlet, they shall be as white as snow; though they are red like crimson, they shall be as wool" (Isa. 1:18b).[3]

It is easy to overlook or give short shrift to the process of confession and repentance of sin. Besides the fact that it is often an unpleasant process that we would rather ignore, we are so eager to pursue the "good stuff" of the anointing that we short circuit the process when we do not deal adequately with the sin and uncleanliness in our lives. Don't pass over this step lightly!

The third step to receiving the anointing is to ask the Heavenly Father to anoint you and fill you afresh with the power of the Holy Spirit. Often we do not have because we have not asked. "So I say to you, ask, and it will be given to you; seek and you will find; knock, and it will be opened to you. For everyone who asks receives, and he who seeks finds, and to him who knocks it will be opened" (Luke 11:9-10).[4]

At the beginning of this chapter, I shared with you how I became so discouraged at the lack of true spiritual power in my ministry that I was ready to quit. I knew there had to be more, so I began a personal quest for the Holy Spirit. It was quite a journey. First I went to my best friend, a Bible teacher who I loved and respected, and asked him if he knew how to get filled with the Holy Spirit. He said he thought it came by the laying on of hands. So he laid hands on me and prayed for me, but all it did was muss up my hair. That wasn't the way.

My next stop in my quest was going to seminary. Seeking counsel from one of the theological experts at the school, I cited the verses in Mark chapter 16 about the signs that would follow those who believed. He patted me on the head, like a puppy, and told me those verses weren't supposed to be in the Bible—that they were a later addition. Then he advised me to leave those verses alone or else they would "mess up" my ministry. He was right. My ministry needed to be messed up! I didn't find the answer to my quest at seminary.

Then I thought I would try the Pentecostal church. After all, Pentecostals had the Holy Spirit, didn't they? A Southern Baptist preacher going to the Pentecostals? Hey, I was desperate! I had never been in a service like that before. Everybody was whooping and hollering and singing and shouting. It was pretty vibrant in that place. The preacher really preached up a storm and afterward, when he was standing at the front, I went down to him and said, "My name's Bobby Connor. I'm a southern Baptist pastor. I've come because I'm looking for the Holy Ghost." The place went nuts! The pastor fell over, leaving me standing there. People in the congregation jumped up and started running around the church whooping and hollering and dancing. They threw me down over the prayer altar. I mean, they were all over me. I finally crawled under the piano bench and asked them to leave me alone so I could pray! So I said, "Lord?" He said, "Get up, Bobby, this is not Me." So I got up and left. I still didn't have my answer.

I had gone to my best friend, I had gone to seminary, and I had gone to the Pentecostal church looking for the Holy Spirit. I had been on this quest for weeks. While driving home, I prayed, "Lord Jesus, what do I do?" He said, "I've been waiting for this." He brought to my mind Luke 11:13, where Jesus says, "If you then, being evil, know how to give good gifts to your children, how much more will your heavenly Father give the Holy Spirit to those who ask Him!"

So I asked Him. The Holy Spirit fell on me. "What happened?" you ask? I'll tell you exactly what happened. I began to develop a wonderful appreciation for the Word of God. It was like a geyser, like an overflow of life. God's Word was no longer just something I studied to prepare a sermon. It was an absolute love letter from God feeding my life. One thing I have learned, you can't have the power of God if you're afraid of the Spirit of God. Do you want God to anoint you? Ask Him.

The fourth step to receiving and walking in the anointing is to start confessing what God's Word has to say about you—instead of confessing how you feel. Confess confidence in Christ's ability in you. Learn to speak not what you feel, but what God's Word teaches. If you see yourself as weak and unworthy and not fit for service, that is exactly how the enemy will see you.

What you think about yourself determines how you will act. Our beliefs always affect our behavior. Proverbs 23:7a says, "For as he thinks in his heart, so is he." We must fill our hearts with faith, not fear. Remember, faith comes by hearing the Word of God. "So then faith comes by hearing, and hearing by the word of God" (Rom. 10:17).[5]

One of the most encouraging words the Lord has ever spoken to me was when He said, "Now people are getting power hungry for all the right reasons." Power hungry for all the right reasons. Why do we want the anointing? Is it so that people will look at us and say, "Oh, he (or she) has the anointing"? No. We want the anointing so that people will look at us but see Christ! That's what we have to do to walk in true anointing: put Christ on display in our lives. Paul said, "But we all, with unveiled face, beholding as in a mirror the glory of the Lord, are being transformed into the same image from glory to glory, just as by the Spirit of the Lord" (2 Cor. 3:18). We are being transformed from glory into glory. The New International Version says we're changed "into His likeness with ever-increasing glory." Isn't that what you want? Don't you want the presence and power of Christ in your life so completely that when people look at you, they will not see you but will see Christ in you? That's what the anointing is all about.

NOTES

1. Bobby Conner, *Understanding the Anointing* (Moravian Falls, NC: Demonstration of God's Power, 2003), 3-6.

2. Bobby Conner, *Understanding the Anointing*, 23.

3. *Ibid.*, 24.

4. *Ibid.*, 24.

5. *Ibid.*, 24-25.

CHAPTER 8

Walking in the Anointing

Receiving the anointing is one thing; walking in it is another. Discontent with empty religion and the status quo may have made you desperately hungry for a fresh move of God in your life. In your desperation, you have examined your heart—and asked God to examine it—and you have dealt with any sin or other hindrance found there through confession and repentance. Now, in the assurance of the purifying and cleansing work of the Spirit in your heart, you have asked God to anoint you and fill you afresh with the Holy Spirit's power. You have begun confessing what God's Word says about you with confidence in Christ's ability in you. And God has given you His anointing—a fresh touch of His Spirit.

Now what? How do you maintain this fresh, wonderful anointing that you have received? How do you walk in it day-by-day and keep it fresh and new and powerful in your life? Above all, keep in mind that just as you did not receive the anointing through your own wisdom or power, you also cannot maintain it or walk in it in your own strength alone. Walking in the anointing is a lifestyle of humility—of complete and utter dependence on God.

Nevertheless, there are several attitudes or character traits that will help you stay in the necessary spiritual posture to walk consistently in the anointing. We will look at four: accessibility, teachability, restorability, and availability.

Accessibility

Those who would walk in the anointing must be accessible, not only to God but also to other people. If there is one thing the Gospels make clear about Jesus Christ, it is that He was accessible. Jesus was on a vitally important mission from His Father—to proclaim the coming of the Kingdom of God and to die for the sin of man so that we could enter it—and He never allowed Himself to be diverted from that mission. At the same time, He was never too busy to touch, heal, and minister to anyone who came to Him.

Have you ever known leaders, even Christian leaders, who have gotten so big and so important (or self-important, as is usually the case) that they are beyond the reach of the "ordinary" person? That's the "superstar syndrome," and it has no place in Christian discipleship. God prefers to use ordinary folks like you and me. Walking in the anointing means remembering that we are ordinary people carrying an extraordinary anointing from an extraordinary God to carry out extraordinary things.

Some people, once they receive any degree of the anointing, suddenly become inaccessible. They get too close to the anointing, glorying in the anointing instead of in the One who gives the anointing. And they shut themselves off from the "less fortunate" who have not been "touched" as they have.

One of the fastest ways to shut down the anointing is to allow ourselves to get too big for our britches. If we are full of ourselves, we cannot be full of the anointing. Remember, this is not about us, but about Him—it is all about Him!

Even Jesus never claimed to do anything on His own. He said and did only what He saw His Father saying and doing (see John 5:19; 8:26). And He was always accessible. He loved and welcomed children near Him, and He blessed them. On at least one occasion, He rebuked His disciples for trying to send them away (see Matt. 19:13-15). Jesus willingly and openly associated with "tax collectors and sinners" (see Matt. 9:10-13), the unclean, the castoff, the dregs of society—the very people who needed Him most and who were ignored by everybody else. Although ridiculed and criticized by the self-righteous in society, Jesus was not afraid of losing His reputation. Why not? Because He willingly "made Himself of no reputation" in order to win our salvation. And as His disciples, we are to do the same. Paul put it this way:

> *Let this mind be in you which was also in Christ Jesus, who, being in the form of God, did not consider it robbery to be equal with God, but made Himself of no reputation, taking the form of a bondservant, and coming in the likeness of men. And being found in appearance as a man, He humbled Himself and became obedient to the point of death, even the death of the cross* (Philippians 2:5-8).

Jesus could not have done this without making Himself accessible. And we cannot walk consistently in the anointing without being accessible too. We cannot be so protective of our dignity and reputation or so fearful of being vulnerable that we close ourselves off from others.

One day, while passing through Jericho, Jesus stopped at the foot of a large sycamore tree. He looked up at the small man who was gazing down at him from its branches and said, "Zacchaeus, make haste and come down, for today I must stay at your house" (Luke 19:5b). Zacchaeus was thrilled and hurried down, but the crowd around Jesus was scandalized. Why? Zacchaeus was a crooked collaborator. As a tax collector for the Romans, he routinely cheated his own people to line his own pockets. Little wonder that they hated him. And many of the upright citizens of Jericho were offended when Jesus chose to stay with such a man.

Zacchaeus represents all of those people who live a shady life and are hungry for God but don't want anybody to know they're hungry. Being a short man, Zacchaeus climbed the sycamore tree so he could see Jesus, but he didn't want anyone to see the hunger in his heart. Not, at least, until Jesus called him. Then he didn't care. He scrambled out of that tree and received Jesus with joy, not only into his home but also into his heart. Look what happened:

> Then Zacchaeus stood and said to the Lord, "Look, Lord, I give half of my goods to the poor; and if I have taken anything from anyone by false accusation, I restore fourfold." And Jesus said to him, "Today salvation has come to this house, because he also is a son of Abraham; for the Son of Man has come to seek and to save that which was lost" (Luke 19:8-10).

Zacchaeus's life and eternal destiny were transformed forever. But it never would have happened if Jesus had not made Himself accessible. Accessibility was key to Jesus' mission, which was "to seek and to save that which was lost." He could not do that without going to where the lost could be found. He could not do it without being accessible. The more accessible we are, the more God will be able to use us to touch and transform the lives of others. If you want to walk in the anointing, be accessible.

Teachability

Along with accessibility comes teachability, a teachable spirit. Just because you carry the anointing does not mean you have nothing else to learn. On the contrary, a disciple is always learning—that's the meaning of the word disciple. Many people today, including many in the Church, seem to display an attitude that there is nothing anyone can teach them, especially those of an earlier and older generation. Unless it's brand new and completely fresh, they don't want it. To be sure, God is always doing something new, and we always need a fresh anointing, but the anointing and the new things that God does are always about His eternal Kingdom and the timeless gospel of Christ—things that never change. So we need both the old and the new. And we need humble spirits that are willing to learn from those who can teach us.

In my first pastorate, many years ago, I was a young, strapping, wild sort of guy, strong as an ox. And one of my church members was old Mr. Clayton. Skinny, wiry, and in his early 70s, Mr. Clayton had bodily strength that belied his age and size. I discovered this one day when we went to cut down some trees on a plot of land where we were going to construct a new church building. The trees needed to go in order to give a survey team access to take measurements.

Mr. Clayton got his long-handled axe out of his car and went to work. He'd go whack, and that axe cut deep into that tree with every stroke. In minutes, the tree was down and he moved on to another. After felling several trees, he stopped and wiped his brow with a handkerchief. I'd been watching all of this and, knowing I was strong, said to him, "Mr. Clayton, give me that axe. Let me do some of the work."

He looked at me and asked, "Do you know how to use an axe?"

"Sure,"I replied."I know how to use an axe." I walked over to a sapling, a little tree no more than two or three inches in diameter, and I was going to show Mr. Clayton how well I could use that axe. Putting my back into it, I took a mighty swing—and missed. I gnarled up the axe handle a little, and Mr. Clayton gave me a look that said, "Boy you don't know nothing about axes do you?" I took one more swing and nearly broke the axe handle. That's when he took it back from me and went back to work. I was strong, but strength alone wasn't enough. I also needed knowledge. There was a lot I needed to learn from Mr. Clayton.

When I was in high school, I used to make some extra money loading watermelons. Some of my friends and I, all of us football players, would go to the farmers' market where the farmers brought their watermelons in on trucks, and we were paid to transfer the melons from the trucks to train boxcars. It was a good physical workout for us and helped us stay in shape, and we got paid besides, so what wasn't to like?

Those were the days when farmers grew really large water-melons, much larger than what you usually find today. One of us would pick up a melon, carry it over and hand it to the next guy in line, who would carry it to the next guy, and so on until the last one loaded it onto the boxcar.

This went on for a little while, and the whole time an old guy sat watching us from under a tree next to the courthouse. He was as skinny as a lizard. After watching us for a while, he walked over, spat out a big brown wad of chewing tobacco on the ground and said, "You boys don't know nothing about loading melons do ya?"

"What do you mean?" I answered. "Sure we can load water-melons."

"Not very well."

"I suppose you can load them, with those scrawny little arms of yours?"

He said, "I can load them better than you can."

I doubted it, but said, "OK, show us."

And he did. He was right; he could load them better than we could! The secret he taught us was in how to let loose of the melon. We had been doing it wrong. I would pick up a melon, give it to Randy, who would give it to Thomas, and so on. That's not how you load watermelons. The way you load watermelons is by picking them up and tossing them. Instead of carrying it, you just pitch it to the next person in line. Then it becomes easy. From the momentum of my toss, Randy would catch it and pitch it to Thomas in one smooth motion. It's all in the knowing how. And sometimes we learn from the most unlikely teachers.

I believe many of us struggle with our burdens the way Randy, Thomas, and I struggled with those watermelons. By the time that skinny, old man was finished with us, we could load watermelons all day long and never get a sore back. He was like the Holy Spirit, teaching us a better way. A teachable spirit requires humility. And instead of carrying our burdens, we are supposed to cast them on the Lord. As Peter counsels us, "Therefore humble yourselves under the mighty hand of God, that He may exalt you in due time, casting all your care upon Him, for He cares for you" (1 Pet. 5:6-7). We have to learn to let loose of our burdens and let the momentum carry them away.

Without a teachable spirit, we will never be able to sustain the anointing because it comes from the Spirit of God, who is our Teacher. Jesus said, "But the Helper, the Holy Spirit, whom the Father will send in My name, He will teach you all things, and bring to your remembrance all things that I said to you" (John 14:26). Be teachable, and the Lord will teach you. Just don't be surprised at who He sends to do the job!

Restorability

Another vital mindset for walking in the anointing is the attitude of restorability. Because we are sinners saved by grace, we are not perfect. We will make mistakes. At times, we will yield to temptation. We will slip into sin. Restorability means understanding that while some failure along the way is inevitable, failure is never final. There is always a way back. Just as any believer who is hungry and desperate for the anointing can receive it, any believer who has fallen or who has stepped out from under the anointing can be restored. God is able and willing to bring restoration. He does not will that any of His children be isolated from Him or relegate themselves to lives of defeat and frustration.

The restoration of the anointing can be illustrated by an event in the life of the Old Testament prophet Elisha.

And the sons of the prophets said to Elisha, "See now, the place where we dwell with you is too small for us. Please, let us go to the Jordan, and let every man take a beam from there, and let us make there a place where we may dwell." So he answered, "Go." Then one said, "Please consent to go with your servants." And he answered, "I will go." So he went with them. And when they came to the Jordan, they cut down trees. But as one was cutting down a tree, the iron ax head fell into the water; and he cried out and said, "Alas, master! For it was borrowed." So the man of God said, "Where did it fall?" And he showed him the place. So he cut off a stick, and threw it in there; and he made the iron float. Therefore he said, "Pick it up for yourself." So he reached out his hand and took it (2 Kings 6:1-7).

The "sons of the prophets" were prophets in training and Elisha was their teacher. They decided they needed bigger lodgings, so they asked Elisha for permission to cut down trees at the Jordan River to use in building new quarters. When Elisha granted permission, one of the students asked him to accompany them, and Elisha consented. Like Jesus several centuries later, Elisha was accessible. The leader went with his students. He did not abandon them to their own devices. The prophetic is more caught than taught. Just get around it long enough and it kind of rubs off on you.

The stage is being set for a miracle. One of these prophets in training was cutting down a tree next to the river, and the ax head fell off into the water. Maybe he got distracted or didn't know how to use an ax (where's Mr. Clayton when you need him!), but for some reason unknown to us, the axe head fell off the handle. There wasn't much he could do with only an ax handle. He could have played games. He could have said, "I'm going to continue to hit and act like I'm working. Maybe nobody will notice that my tree is not falling."

That represents empty religious activity, useless busyness, which is where much of the Church is today. Swinging and sweating, but with no trees falling—never aware that their ax has lost its handle. Why? Because we've lost the anointing.

To his everlasting credit, however, this young prophet-to-be was not content to go through the motions. What about you? Aren't you tired of going through the motions? Aren't you tired of a lot of swinging and sweating and striving and keeping up a good appearance? Look what this young man did. He called to Elisha, "Alas, master, for it was borrowed." Whenever we forget that the gift is from God and start acting like it belongs to us, we can lose it. Any anointing we receive comes from God, not from our own initiative. As James says, "Every good gift and every perfect gift is from above, and comes down from the

Father of lights, with whom there is no variation or shadow of turning" (James 1:17).

I love Elishas's response: "Where did it fall?" Where did we lose the anointing? Where did we become separated from the power of God? Perhaps it was when we began to compromise with political agendas. Maybe we lost it because of the fear of men, becoming more concerned about what others think than about what God wants. Or perhaps the anointing departed when sin entered our hearts and pushed it out. Whatever the reason, we have to come to grips with where it fell.

When Elisha asked, "Where did it fall?" the man showed him the spot. He knew exactly where he had been standing when the ax head fell off. We can't be looking in all the wrong places for restoration of what we need. We have to know where we lost it and return to that place to find it again. And we have to be honest with ourselves and with God. If we're going to experience a restoration of power and the anointing, we're going to have to get brazenly and boldly honest. The man could have tried to cover himself and say, "I don't know where I lost it." And he would have missed his blessing. Instead, he was honest and experienced a miracle.

Elisha took a stick, cast it into the water over the spot where the ax head had disappeared, and the iron ax head floated. I believe that stick represents the cross of Christ. Through the cross, Christ restores to us everything that we've lost. Imagine the young prophet's amazement when Elisha threw the stick in and the water started gurgling and bubbling and then the ax head suddenly bobbed to the surface! That which he feared was lost forever was restored. He regained his ability to perform the job that God had assigned to him.

Notice too that Elisha did not retrieve the ax head and put it back on the handle. Instead, he instructed his student, "Pick it up for yourself." I think this is a very important point. This is the same thing we're going to have to do in our churches. The prophets are going to have to do what God calls them to do. We're going to have to find out where we lost the power of God, and then they're going to have to say, "Pick it up for yourself." Personally, I believe that when this student picked up the ax head and put it back on the handle—when his power and anointing were restored—he felled more trees than all the rest of them. I think he made every stroke count. IIe had been restored. He had a second chance, and I believe he made the most of it.

Wisdom is always better than might. If we want restoration, if we want to walk in the anointing consistently, we have to believe in miracles. We have to believe that God can restore to the Church what has been lost due to sin, ignorance, compromise, and unbelief.

Here's another interesting point: the ax head fell into the Jordan River. In the Bible, the Jordan River often represents that which stands in the way of the people of God receiving what He has promised. One particular feature of the Jordan River is that it overflows its banks at harvest time. Yet, in the Book of Joshua, that was the time of year when God commanded Joshua and the Israelites to cross the Jordan into Canaan, the Promised Land. He instructed them to cross at the precise time when the river was at its widest and deepest point and when its current was at its fastest.

Have you ever noticed how God often directs us to advance at the most inopportune times? We'd rather wait until after harvest time, when the water goes down, but God prefers that we advance under the most adverse situations. Why? So that He can receive the glory. He wants to leave no doubt in anyone's mind as to who did it. God is glorified when the world sees us do something beyond our power to do, something that only God can do.

When the Israelites got ready to cross the Jordan, the priests bearing the ark of the covenant led the way. As the priests stepped into the waters of the river, the water rolled up all the way back to the city of Adam and the children of Israel went across on dry ground (see Josh. 3:14-17).

Whatever your personal Jordan may be, whatever stands between you and what God promised you, God can move it out of the way. He can make a way when it seems like there is no way. We have to believe that we can be restored. We have to believe that we can recover what the enemy stole from us. God wants to restore it. He wants to restore you if you need restoring. Aren't you tired of just swinging the handle with no head?

One of the saddest verses in the Bible is Jeremiah 8:20: "The harvest is past, the summer is ended, and we are not saved!" We don't want that to happen. We don't want to miss the day of our visitation. God is asking us the question, "Where did it fall?" Where did we really begin to wane in our walk with the Lord? And why? We have to come clean and be brutally honest. It won't do to simply shrug our shoulders and say, "I don't know." If we ask the Lord, He'll show us where we departed from Him. James says:

> If any of you lacks wisdom, let him ask of God, who gives to all liberally and without reproach, and it will be given to him. But let him ask in faith, with no doubting, for he who doubts is like a wave of the sea driven and tossed by the wind. For let not that man suppose that he will receive anything from the Lord; he is a double-minded man, unstable in all his ways (James 1:5-8).

Remember, failure is never final. But we must believe in our restorability and in His power and willingness to restore. And He is willing. There is always a way back into the grace and favor and anointing and power of the Lord. He's always calling us back.

Availability

If walking in the anointing means being accessible to people, it also means being available to God. This calls for an attitude of humility, recognizing how utterly dependent we are upon Him. People who feel self-sufficient in their own strength do not make themselves available to God because they don't see the need. God calls the ordinary, the outcasts, the desperate, and the destitute. He calls the very people who know that without Him they don't have a prayer. God calls the "Jephthahs" of the world.

On the Day of Atonement a few years ago, I had a vision where the Lord Jesus appeared in the doorway. A bright light shone from behind Him. He said, "Bobby, I want you to meet your brother." My only brother was killed by lightning on May 29, 1979, so I thought this word from the Lord was quite strange. Then He gestured with His hand as if introducing someone, and a figure stepped through the doorway. And the Lord said, "Meet your brother Jephthah."

Jephthah was an outcast, the son of a harlot, driven off by his half-brothers, the legitimate sons of their common father. He also had a reputation as a "mighty man of valor." His story is recorded in the 11th chapter of the Book of Judges. Denied his inheritance because of his parentage, Jephthah knew what it was to suffer bitter, horrible betrayal. Years later, however, when those same brothers stood in need of a valiant champion, they turned to Jephthah.

When the Ammonites invaded and made trouble for Israel, Jephthah's people, the Gileadites, brought him back from exile and asked him to lead them. After understandably questioning why they came to him (since they had thrown him out), and after receiving assurances from them that he would not be cast out again, Jephthah stepped up as the leader and the liberator of the children of Israel. He overcame bitter betrayal. God is going to do that again. Today there are many Jephthahs outside the door who have been cast out by self-righteous brothers. And God's going to bring them back in.

The first thing Jephthah did was to talk to the enemy. He tried to negotiate with words, and they wouldn't negotiate. Then he said, "How dare you come and violate my land?" Very quickly he re-associated himself with his brothers. He called it his land, his inheritance. The very land that he had been kicked off of and the very inheritance that he had been denied were his again. When the opportunity for restoration came, Jephthah made himself available.

God's going to bring in the outcasts. Some of God's very best leaders are not in the Church right now; they've been cast out. But God is in the process of calling them back in, and we'd better get ready for them. Some of the strongest leaders will be people we've never heard of. They're going to come to the front so quickly that our heads are going to spin.

Who knows? Maybe you will be one of them! Don't forget that God can anoint anyone and use anyone for any purpose He desires. If it serves His purpose, He can exalt any one of us higher than we could ever imagine, or He can use us in places where only a few will ever know who we are. The place of service and level of notoriety are not important, being available to the Lord for whatever purpose He chooses is.

One of the things we need to understand is that, when we get the Holy Spirit, He can give you any gift He wills. I've heard that we shouldn't seek after spiritual things, yet the Bible tells us specifically to desire spiritual gifts (see 1 Cor. 14:1). We should seek after them and pursue them. Some people even say that we shouldn't talk about the supernatural.

Hundreds of verses in the Bible talk about the supernatural, and it tells us to expect miracles.

As disciples who want to walk consistently in the anointing, we need to make ourselves available for the Holy Spirit to give us any gift He wishes. I've seen some people who hold out for a specific gift. They are unwilling to work or serve unless it is in the specific area that they desire. With that attitude, they will never walk in the anointing and never know the joy and satisfaction of being used of God. For my part, I'll take any gift the Spirit wants to give me, anyway He chooses to give it! I want to be available. The Bible says that the Spirit imparts gifts as He chooses (see 1 Cor. 12:11). We have the potential to receive any gift, but the choice of gift is His, not ours. Our part is to make ourselves available.

With the Holy Spirit living inside you, any gift that He has is available to you. If you are drawn to a particular gift, which you see operating in someone else, ask the Lord for it. Then position your heart, allowing for His sovereignty and ultimate will. I believe that, in many cases, He will give it to you if you are willing to do what the person in whom you saw it operating did to get it. Many times we look at somebody walking under an anointing or walking under a real grace of God and we think, "Oh man, I want that." Are you willing to do what they did to get it?

The anointing is for you if you have the passion and the hunger for it. It is a sovereign work of God in your life to prepare you for service and ministry. Philippians 2:13 says, "For it is God who works in you both to will and to do for His good pleasure." God Himself works in us to give us the will to work for Him. We don't just wake up one day and decide on our own to do something great for God. No, it is God who wills it and who works it in us. He is the one who qualifies and not us. The Holy Spirit comes inside of us and anoints us to do any task that God assigns to us. We have to quit feeling like we're inferior for the task. Instead, we need to start saying, "I'm well able." We need to agree with Paul when he says, "I can do all things through Christ who strengthens me" (Phil. 4:13).

Affirming our ability, as God makes us able, puts us in company with Caleb. Remember him? He and Joshua alone of the generation of Israelites that left Egypt lived to enter the Promised Land because they remained faithful to believe in and act on God's promises. When finally, at the age of eighty-five, Caleb was ready to claim the inheritance for which he had waited so long, he said, "As yet I am as strong this day as on the day that Moses sent me; just as my strength was then, so now is my strength for war, both for going out and for coming in" (Josh. 14:11).

Caleb's name means "salty old dog, tenacious one." The one who won't let go. Be like Caleb. Don't let go of your dream no matter what. Whatever God has promised you, hang on to that promise. Remain faithful, tenacious, and available, and He will bring to pass everything He promised you. Though it may seem long in coming, don't cast it away.

It says in Hebrews:

> *Therefore do not cast away your confidence, which has great reward. For you have need of endurance, so that after you have done the will of God, you may receive the promise: "For yet a little while, and He who is coming will come and will not tarry. Now the just shall live by faith; but if anyone draws back, My soul has no pleasure in him"* (Hebrews 10:35-38).

"Don't cast away your confidence, which has great reward." One translation says, "Don't fling away from you this lively hope." Don't give up or give in to discouragement if things do not happen in the timing or manner that you prefer. Let God choose the manner and the timing. His will is always best. Many people think that they're going to get a prophetic anointing and—snap—it will come just that fast. Most of the time it doesn't work that way. God promised the children of Israel an inheritance in a land flowing with milk and honey. Then He led them out of Egypt into the desert. Did God lie? No, the Bible says He led them into the desert to test their hearts (see Deut. 8:2). And most of them failed the test. They complained to Moses, "Why did you bring us out here to die? It would have been better if we had stayed in Egypt" (see Exod. 16:3).

Don't long for Egypt. Don't look back to what once was. Your future lies ahead of you. Your destiny awaits. The only direction is forward. Be accessible. Be teachable. Be restorable. Be available. Step into the anointing that God has for you, and walk in it with Him! It's what you were born to do!

CHAPTER

The Church's Finest Hour

There is nothing like the deep and confident faith of a little child. Once during a meeting, I looked out across the congregation and saw a little boy with a heart-breaking deformity. For some reason, his forehead had never developed properly, and it swept almost straight back just above his eyes, causing them to stick out more like those of an animal than a human.

During the ministry time, this precious little boy came forward for prayer. He wanted to ask the Lord to heal him. Before I prayed for him, I questioned him. We were standing in front of a whole congregation full of people. Everyone in the room could see and hear everything that was going on. I asked him, "Son, do you believe Jesus can do this? Do you believe Jesus can heal you?"

He looked up at me with that pathetically, tragically malformed head and those protruding, animal-like eyes and said in a bold voice, "I'm here, ain't I?"

What an answer! Never in all my years of preaching and ministry have I received a better answer or a finer expression of faith in the healing power of the Lord. "I'm here, ain't I?" That pretty much says it all!

After hearing that wonderful response from this little boy, I laid my hands on him and prayed for him. He fell over under the power of the Spirit, and when he got up a few minutes later, God had already begun to rotate and grow out the bones in his forehead! I could see it happening right in front of me!

Several months later, my wife and I returned to that church. This same little boy and his mother came up to greet us. The restructuring of his face had continued until he now looked almost completely normal. He had also grown several inches. He was so elated, so happy about what the Lord Jesus Christ had done for him.

"I'm here, ain't I?" This little boy believed Jesus could heal him and acted on that belief. And he was healed. That's what we need today, people who will believe God to the point of action. Kathryn Kuhlman said, "When people's faith gets to the point of action, something has to happen."

God Is So Good

Grownups often ignore or dismiss the words and beliefs of children as immature or foolish, but not Jesus. One day, when His disciples tried to turn away those who were bringing their children to Him,

> ...[Jesus] *was greatly displeased and said to them, "Let the little children come to Me, and do not forbid them; for of such is the Kingdom of God. Assuredly, I*

say to you, whoever does not receive the Kingdom of God as a little child will by no means enter it." And He took them up in His arms, laid His hands on them, and blessed them (Mark 10:14-16).

Much more than most adults, children are willing to take God at His word. In the mind of a child, if God said it, that settles it. That kind of faith comes naturally to a child, but we grownups have to work at it. Why is childlike faith so hard for us? The hardening of our hearts and minds due to sin is one reason. Another is that we simply don't trust God. We're not confident that He truly has our best interest at heart. This is the same problem the human race has struggled with ever since the Garden of Eden when satan first sowed seeds of doubt in Eve's mind about God's integrity. Not only that, but so many adults have been fed so many lies about God and have developed so many completely erroneous ideas about God that they cannot even see Him for the God of love that He is.

In these days that we are living in, the world needs to see, to learn, to know that God is good and that God is love and that He is for us and not against us. And we who make up the Church in this generation have a greater opportunity than any previous generation to show this great and awesome God of love to the world. With the new thing that God is doing in our midst, I believe we are heading into days that will be the Church's finest hour.

One of my favorite verses in the Bible is Nahum 1:7: "The Lord is good, a stronghold in the day of trouble; and He knows those who trust in Him." The Lord is good. Goodness is God's very nature. And the goodness of God is what the Church needs to declare and demonstrate before the world. Why? Because the truth of God's goodness has been under attack ever since Eden. We need to declare the goodness of God's nature, the goodness of His grace, the goodness of His mercy, the goodness of His love, and the goodness of His justice and judgment. God demonstrated His goodness beyond all dispute when He sent His Son, Jesus Christ, to die on the cross for our sins. God judged our sins at Calvary, laying the penalty on His Son so that we could be forgiven and set free. In a generation that is rapidly rejecting the very concept of absolute truth, the Church of Jesus Christ must boldly declare and demonstrate to the world the objective truths that God is good, that God is love, and that Christ is Lord.

Heaven will be wonderful, but God wants to show us good this side of Heaven too. He wants to show Himself strong on behalf of those whose hearts belong to Him (see 2 Chron. 16:9). He always stands ready to help us: "God is our refuge and strength, a very present help in trouble" (Ps. 46:1). "I will lift up my eyes to the hills—from whence comes my help? My help comes from the Lord, who made Heaven and earth" (Ps. 121:1-2). God is both accessible and available, and the world needs to see that truth revealed in us, the Church. They need to see it in our attitudes and our lifestyles. The Church in its finest hour will live in such a way that, when people look at us, they will see God. Jesus said, "Let your light so shine before men, that they may see your good works and glorify your Father in Heaven" (Matt. 5:16).

Seeing from God's Perspective

Knowing that God is good changes our whole perspective of the world, particularly with regard to the suffering and sorrow of humanity. In recent years, we have witnessed an alarming array of troubles, from school shootings and terrorist attacks to deadly natural disasters like the "Christmas" tsunami of December 2004 and Hurricanes Katrina and Rita in 2005. Everywhere I go, people have asked me, "What does it all mean, Bobby? Are we under God's judgment?" I had the same questions, so I asked the Lord. This is what He told me:

"Bobby, tell My people that I love them too deeply to allow them to continue living the way they are living." What we're going through now is more of a correction than a judgment.

Even God's "correction" is evidence of His goodness, no matter how unpleasant it may be for us at the time. God is trying to get our attention. He is trying to turn us around, get our eyes off of ourselves and onto Him so that we can see things from His perspective. And He always begins with His own people. Our calling as anointed disciples of the Lord is to make an invisible God visible—to display the likeness of Christ in our own lives. But how can we do that if we are not looking at Him? We must learn to accept—and even welcome—God's corrective actions in our lives so that we can fulfill our calling and point others to Christ. Simon Peter put it this way:

> For the time has come for judgment to begin at the house of God; and if it begins with us first, what will be the end of those who do not obey the gospel of God? Now "If the righteous one is scarcely saved, where will the ungodly and the sinner appear?" Therefore let those who suffer according to the will of God commit their souls to Him in doing good, as to a faithful Creator (1 Peter 4:17-19).

Perspective is everything. Father God wants us to see from His perspective downward, not upward from the world's perspective. This is why Jesus taught us to pray to the Father, "Your kingdom come. Your will be done on earth as it is in Heaven" (Matt. 6:10). From the world's point of view, nothing is sure or certain, but from God's viewpoint, everything He wills is already accomplished. The anointing gives us God's perspective because it connects us intimately with His heart, mind, will, and purpose. From that vantage point, we can proceed in complete confidence, knowing that our future is as certain as the promises of God. The world needs to see that certainty, and it is the calling of the Church to reveal it.

Too many Christians either have lost God's perspective or never had it to start with. When measured against the "giants" of naturalistic science, worldly culture, and postmodern philosophy, many of us who are believers feel powerless and helpless and on the defensive. Like the Israelites in the 13th chapter of Numbers, we see ourselves as "grasshoppers" in comparison. If that is the way we see ourselves, then that is the way the world will see us.

Learning to see from God's perspective gets rid of the "grasshopper syndrome." From that vantage point, we can see that the "giants" of human wisdom, culture, and philosophy are really insignificant grasshoppers next to the power, plan, and purpose of God. It is time for the Church to rise up in holy confidence and assurance. We need to perceive ourselves as bold and strong in Christ. We need to get our eyes off of our circumstances and look to Jesus, "the Author and Finisher of our faith" (see Heb. 12:2a). From His eternal perspective, we can see that no matter how big the problem is, Jesus is always bigger. The anointing helps us to gain and maintain this godly perspective.

Hearing God's Voice

Walking in the anointing not only enables us to see from God's perspective, it also increases our sensitivity and ability to hear His voice. God speaks to us in many ways: through circumstances, His Word, prayer, the Holy Spirit, and other believers. Our problem is that so few of us really are conditioned even to expect, much less to listen for, God to speak. This is especially true in the area of prayer.

For many people, including many Christians, prayer is a one-way transmission, a constant litany of requests, petitions, and even demands made of God with little or no thought to what God might want to say in return. We are like a two-way radio with the receiver turned off; we transmit fine but miss completely any messages sent to us.

God never intended prayer to be a monologue where one person (usually us) does all the talking. True prayer is a dialogue, two-way communication between a Father and the children He loves. I love Jeremiah 33:3, where God says, "Call to Me, and I will answer you, and show you great and mighty things, which you do not know." Father God invites us to talk to Him. He longs to hear our voices, and He promises to answer. By talking to God, I don't mean the continual stream of complaints, petitions, and requests that constitute "prayer" for so many of us, although these are certainly appropriate in their place. Prayer is conversation with God, where we talk to Him and He to us, where He listens to us and we to Him. It is in the listening to God part where most of us drop the ball.

Prayer uncovers the deep and mystical things of God. Deuteronomy 29:29 says, "The secret things belong to the Lord our God, but those things which are revealed belong to us and to our children forever, that we may do all the words of this law." The secret things belong to the Lord. But there are many things He wants to reveal to His children, and prayer is one of the ways that He does it. Prayer is a dialogue between friends. Jesus told His disciples, "No longer do I call you servants, for a servant does not know what his master is doing; but I have called you friends, for all things that I heard from My Father I have made known to you" (John 15:15).

Prayer should be a pleasure, not a pressure. It's always a pleasure to talk to somebody we love, to draw near and share intimate conversation. We should look at prayer as a great opportunity rather than as a burden, something we freely choose to do rather than something we perform out of habit or a sense of duty.

Religion has conditioned most people not to expect to hear from God. Consequently, their prayers are a one-way monologue. Many Christians even have been taught that God does not speak today except through the Bible. And God certainly does speak through His written Word, which is "living and powerful, and sharper than any two-edged sword, piercing even to the division of soul and spirit, and of joints and marrow, and is a discerner of the thoughts and intents of the heart" (Heb. 4:12). We do indeed receive revelation from God's Word as the Holy Spirit gives us illumination in our reading and studying. But there are many other ways that God can communicate.

I once asked the Lord to tell me how He speaks. He responded, "I speak any way I want to." So often we try to squeeze God into a box of our own design and expect Him to speak only within the parameters that we have established. What arrogance! What presumption! What sinful pride! We can't confide God to a box. He's God. He can speak any way He pleases and do anything He desires. God is accountable to no one except Himself.

While evangelism—making Christ known to those who don't know Him—is our primary mission as the Body of Christ, prayer should be our primary activity. Jesus was the greatest preacher who ever lived, yet His disciples never asked Him to teach them to preach. And even though He was the greatest miracle-worker who ever lived, they never asked Him to teach them how to perform miracles. The disciples' one recorded request of Jesus was, "Lord, teach us to pray" (see Luke 11:1). And that should be our request as well.

I believe the disciples asked this because of the powerful results of Jesus' prayers that they had witnessed. They saw how Jesus' prayers connected Him with the Father, and they wanted that same connection. Likewise, we should hunger for the prayer connection that Jesus had, not just to be able to speak to God more effectively but also to be able to hear His reply more easily. Jesus was in constant intimate fellowship with His Father, and prayer flowed between them as naturally as breathing. Nothing improves hearing like intimacy. That's why we have to draw near to the Lord. If we want to make Christ known to those who do not know Him, we have to hear what He is saying and see what He is doing so that we can say and do the same things.

One of the secrets to hearing God's voice is to regain the lost art of "tarrying prayer." Some call it "waiting on the Lord." Whatever it's called, it means taking time to slow down and spend extended periods in the Lord's presence, basking in His love and waiting for Him to speak into our hearts. So often, life comes at us in such a rush that the most we take time for is a two-minute devotional reading (if that) and a 30-second prayer, and we're done. No wonder we have trouble hearing the voice of God!

Any relationship takes time and deliberate effort to develop, and our relationship with the Lord is no different. If you want to walk in the anointing and enjoy intimate dialogue with Him, you have to spend time with Him. The more time you spend with the Lord, the better you will know Him and the easier it will be to hear His voice. The better you know Him, the more you will love Him and take joy in obeying Him. And the more you obey Him and the longer you are with Him, the more like Him you will become. An old hymn says it so well:

> Take time to be holy,
> Speak oft with thy Lord;
> Abide in Him always,
> And feed on His Word:
>
> Make friends of God's children,
> Help those who are weak;

Forgetting in nothing
His blessing to seek.

Take time to be holy,
The world rushes on;
Spend much time in secret
With Jesus alone:

By looking to Jesus
Like Him thou shalt be;
Thy friends in thy conduct
His likeness shall see.
Take time to be holy,
Be calm in thy soul;

Each thought and each motive
Beneath His control;

Thus led by His Spirit
To fountains of love,
Thou soon shalt be fitted
For service above.[1]

Personal holiness is a prerequisite for the anointing and is the product of much time spent with the Lord in prayer and fellowship. Peter said, "But as He who called you is holy, you also be holy in all your conduct, because it is written, 'Be holy, for I am holy'" (1 Pet. 1:15-16). I believe that, in our day, the Lord is calling His people, His Church, back to a level of holiness that we have not seen in several generations, perhaps longer. Imagine what a difference a truly holy and anointed Church will make in a corrupt and sin-darkened world!

The Church Has the Answer

I am convinced that we are entering a period that will prove to be the Church's finest hour. We have the answer that the world so desperately needs, and we must stop apologizing for it. Not long ago, I received a visitation from the Lord in which He said to me, "I'm going to release to you the prophetic words of wisdom that will sustain a weary world."

Isaiah 50:4 says, "The Lord God has given Me the tongue of the learned, that I should know how to speak a word in season to him who is weary. He awakens Me morning by morning, He awakens My ear to hear as the learned." Although this verse appears in a longer passage that clearly refers to Christ, it also is relevant for all who follow Him and who desire to walk in His anointing. As Christ is, so are we. We are called to be like Him.

Certainly we all know our world is weary. Just turn on the television news: war, famine, terrorist attacks, pestilence, starvation, genocide, epidemics, tsunamis, hurricanes, earthquakes, shame, guilt, fear. Yes, the world is weary, but the Church is going to rise to the occasion and experience its finest hour! We're going to step from the wings into the very center of the world's stage with a positive message, a message of power and hope in Christ—power to overcome present circumstances and hope for the future.

God is going to give us "the tongue of the learned" so that we may speak "a word in season to him who is weary." I imagine it will be much as it was with the apostle Paul in Acts chapter 27 when the ship carrying him to Rome to be tried by Caesar was buffeted for two weeks by storms so severe that everyone else on board eventually lost all hope of being saved. Paul then stood in their midst and said:

> *I urge you to take heart, for there will be no loss of life among you, but only of the ship. For there stood by me this night an angel of the God to whom I belong and whom I serve, saying, "Do not be afraid, Paul; you must be brought before Caesar; and indeed God has granted you all those who sail with you."*

Therefore take heart, men, for I believe God that it will be just as it was told me (Acts 27:22-25).

That is how it is going to be with the Church and the world. The Church is going to stand on the storm-tossed deck of this world and say, "Everything is going to be alright because we have a living Lord. Turn to Him and find rest. Turn to Him and find hope. Turn to Him and find salvation." As Christ's anointed servants, we will speak the words of life that He has spoken into our hearts, and people all over the world will know the truth that "man shall not live by bread alone, but by every word that proceeds from the mouth of God" (Matt. 4:4). Jesus Christ Himself is the living Word of God (see John 1:1).

Second Chronicles 20:20b says, "Believe in the Lord your God, and you shall be established; believe His prophets, and you shall prosper." The word for *prosper* in Hebrew means that we will live at God's eye-level for our lives. As we hear and believe the Word of the Lord, we shall be established and firmly grounded in our faith and held under His protection. Those who believe the Word we proclaim, as the Lord's prophets, will be established as well, and all of us will prosper.

Amos 3:7 says, "Surely the Lord God does nothing, unless He reveals His secret to His servants the prophets." What God has called us to do, He will equip us to do. He will reveal to us everything we need to know in order to fulfill His purpose. We will be His heralds, proclaiming across the land and to all nations the heart of God for these days. Ours will be the anointing of the sons of Issachar, who had "understanding of the times, to know what [the people of God] should do" (1 Chron. 12:32a). This is not a time for the Church to play dumb. The Lord told me, "I'm going to change the question mark into an exclamation point." So the Church will have the answer. The Church does have the answer, and it is an answer from the heart of God!

We can rest easy knowing that God has everything under control. One night, before the start of a big conference, I was waiting before the Lord and He said, "Bobby, go out there and tell the people that this whole thing is My idea."

"Do you mean the conference?" I asked.

"No," He replied, "the whole thing."

He was talking about everything: creation, the redemption of man, everything. This whole thing is His idea. He's going to pull it off, and no one will stop Him. God is going to have people who praise Him, people devoted to His dear Son. Jesus paid for it all with His precious, priceless blood, and He's going to get what He paid for.

Great troubles surely lie ahead, but so do great victories. In the midst of it all, the Church will proclaim that the Lord is the answer, and out of our apparent weakness will come great strength, a strength that is not our own. His strength is made perfect, or is perfectly revealed, in our weakness. Like Paul, when we are weak for Christ's sake, we are strong (see 2 Cor. 12:10). This is not a time to be weak, but strong in the strength of the Lord. Joel 3:10 says, "Let the weak say, 'I am strong.'" We need to start speaking this truth into our lives and into our churches, because if we start declaring it, we will start believing it.

Christ is saying to His Church, "I have called you for just such an hour as this." From eternity past, He has foreseen this moment, this generation, these days of trouble, turmoil, conflict, unrest, disaster, and despair, and has raised up a people unto Himself who will light a beacon of life and hope to show a weary world the way to freedom and rest.

Let the Weak Say, "I Am Strong"

In our own strength, we are nothing. Remember, Jesus said, "Abide in Me, and I in you. As the branch cannot bear fruit of itself, unless it abides in the vine, neither can you, unless you abide in Me. I am the vine, you are the branches. He who abides in Me, and I in him, bears much fruit; for without Me you can do nothing" (John 15:4-5). It is only as we learn to abide—to walk and rest in Christ—that we will find strength.

The strength of Christ will enable us to overcome every obstacle and to succeed in every endeavor. Paul's confident claim can be ours as well: "I can do all things through Christ who strengthens me" (Phil. 4:13). God wants us to be strong and to succeed. In fact, He wants us to do three things. He wants us to awake, He wants us to arise, and He wants us to adorn Him. God wants us to look just like Him, to bear His likeness in spirit, mind, and behavior. God wants us to walk in power, and He's going to see that we do it. He is determined to see us walk into our destiny, into the future and the hope that He has laid out for us.

I believe that God is going to re-release in our day the "John the Baptist" anointing of Isaiah:

> *The voice of one crying in the wilderness: "Prepare the way of the Lord; make straight in the desert a highway for our God. Every valley shall be exalted and every mountain and hill brought low; the crooked places shall be made straight and the rough places smooth; the glory of the Lord shall be revealed, and all flesh shall see it together; for the mouth of the Lord has spoken"* (Isaiah 40:3-5).

The prophetic anointing prepares the way for the Lord. I am convinced that God has promised that if we will make the proper preparations, we will behold His glory. God wants to reveal His glory, and He is raising up a people for Himself who will let His glory be seen in and through them. He wants to remove every veil from our eyes so that we can behold Him and become just like Him. Remember Paul's words: "But we all, with unveiled face, beholding as in a mirror the glory of the Lord, are being transformed into the same image from glory to glory, just as by the Spirit of the Lord" (2 Cor. 3:18).

One of the veils the Lord wants to remove is the veil of man-made tradition that teaches people the commandments of men rather than the commandments of God, thus making the Word of God of no effect.

Another veil to be removed is the veil of the fear of men. Fear of men is one of the main reasons that people hold onto meaningless tradition. God wants to remove that fear by filling people's hearts with His love. As First John 4:18 assures us, "There is no fear in love; but perfect love casts out fear...." Instead of being as timid as lambs, we will become as bold as lions. Paul said, "For God has not given us a spirit of fear, but of power and of love and of a sound mind" (2 Tim. 1:7).

Proverbs 29:25 says, "The fear of man brings a snare, but whoever trusts in the Lord shall be safe." God has given us His Spirit to free us from fear and anything else that would hold us back: "Now the Lord is the Spirit; and where the Spirit of the Lord is, there is liberty" (2 Cor. 3:17). The Spirit of the Lord is the Spirit of liberty, and He is the Spirit of truth.

What an exciting time we are living in! We are in a day when God is sharing His truths with us. The Church of Jesus Christ is entering its finest hour. Recently the Lord said to me, "I'm going to release to the Body of Christ three implements." An implement is a special tool designed for a specific task. We must keep these three implements in their proper order or else we will be out of order.

The first implement the Lord is releasing to us is a torch. This speaks of revelation and illumination, an anointing to carry the Word of God and the light of the gospel to all the nations as never before. On the tip of the torch is a flame, which stands for purity: purity of life, of heart, and of the Word of God.

Second is the implement of a scepter, which represents divine authority. Whoever holds the scepter carries the authority. The tip of the scepter represents God's favor, just as it used to in the days when kings would extend the tip of the scepter to those being welcomed into the royal presence. We are ambassadors of Christ, carrying the authority that He has delegated to us by His Spirit.

Finally, there is the implement of a sword, which symbolizes power. It is not the cruel, brutal, wanton, destructive power of war, but the power to overcome the enemy. The power of spiritual discernment. The power of the prophetic. It is the power of the living Word of God, which is "sharper than any two-edged sword, piercing even to the division of soul and spirit, and of joints and marrow, and is a discerner of the thoughts and intents of the heart" (Heb. 4:12).

With these implements in place, the Church will indeed enter its finest hour and prepare the way of the Lord for a new and—who knows?—perhaps final generation!

NOTE

1. William D. Longstaff, "Take Time To Be Holy," c. 1882.

CHAPTER

10

The Ministry of the Spirit

I pastored the First Baptist Church of Bullard, Texas, for nearly 20 years. One Sunday morning, while I was preaching, something quite unusual took place. The Church was packed that morning, and as I preached, I stepped away from the pulpit and came down to the floor in front of it. My wife, who was sitting on the front row, had pulled out a box of Altoids breath mints. I said, "Could I have one of those, please?" She handed me the box. I took one of the breath mints and then asked her, "Would you like one?"

"Well, sure," she replied.

I gave her a breath mint and then the lady seated next to her said, "I would like one, Pastor." So I took one of the mints and just pitched it to her. She caught it easily.

A lady sitting behind them said, "I would like one," so I pitched one to her also. Another person asked for a mint, then another, and another, and I suddenly realized that something supernatural was going on. I could pitch these Altoids to people and they could catch them with the greatest of ease.

A strange sense of bold confidence came over me. In front of all those people in the large sanctuary of the First Baptist Church of Bullard, Texas, I spoke to a young man seated on the next to the last pew, way in the back. I'll call him J.T. I said, "Stand up, J.T., and open your mouth. I'm going to throw this Altoid into your mouth." He stood up and waited, mouth open expectantly. I took one of those little breath mints, about the size of a button, and hurled it across the length of the sanctuary, over the heads of all those people and, so help me, right smack-dab into J.T.'s mouth! Normally I couldn't have thrown that into his mouth in ten trillion tries, but God was doing something special that morning.

Then, out of my mouth came these words from the Lord, "Open your mouth wide, and I will fill it" (Ps. 81:10b).

The official slogan of Altoids is, "Curiously Strong Breath Mints." Breath speaks of spirit, and I believe that God Almighty is giving the Church a strong breath of His Spirit!

We are His children, His chosen ones. We are the Body of Christ on earth, divinely appointed to live in this hour and anointed through His Spirit to manifest His power and His glory before the world. Thus we will make the invisible God visible, and through us, He will draw others to Himself. In this, we will be doing the same work as Christ, our Lord and King, who identified the power and purpose of His mission in these words from Isaiah:

> *The Spirit of the Lord God is upon Me, because the Lord has anointed Me to preach good tidings to the poor; He has sent Me to heal the brokenhearted, to proclaim liberty to the captives, and the opening of the prison to those who are bound; to proclaim the*

acceptable year of the Lord, and the day of vengeance of our God; to comfort all who mourn, to console those who mourn in Zion, to give them beauty for ashes, the oil of joy for mourning, the garment of praise for the spirit of heaviness; that they may be called trees of righteousness, the planting of the Lord, that He may be glorified (Isaiah 61:1-3).

Because we are the Body of Christ, the same Spirit who rested on Him rests on us. Even better, the Spirit of God rests in us; He resides in our hearts as an ever-present Companion. But just exactly who is this Spirit who lives in us? What is His purpose? What are the ministries He carries out in our lives?

The Holy Spirit is Our Comforter

First of all, the Holy Spirit is our constant Companion, through whom we enjoy intimate fellowship with Christ. Jesus called Him the "Helper" and the "Comforter." For three years, Jesus' disciples experienced Jesus' companionship and close physical presence. But what about after He went away? After He died, was resurrected, and ascended back to Heaven, what would happen to His disciples? Jesus promised that He would never leave them alone:

And I will pray the Father, and He will give you another Helper, that He may abide with you forever— the Spirit of truth, whom the world cannot receive, because it neither sees Him nor knows Him; but you know Him, for He dwells with you and will be in you. I will not leave you orphans; I will come to you (John 14:16-18).

The coming of the Holy Spirit as Helper would be more than a temporary, stopgap measure; He would reside permanently inside every believer. It was for this reason, Jesus assured His disciples, that it was better for them for Him to go away; otherwise, the Spirit would not come: "Nevertheless I tell you the truth. It is to your advantage that I go away; for if I do not go away, the Helper will not come to you; but if I depart, I will send Him to you" (John 16:7).

The King James Version and several other translations use the word *Comforter* instead of *Helper* in these and other verses to describe the Holy Spirit. Both words translate the same Greek word, *parakletos*, which also means advocate, intercessor, and consoler. The Holy Spirit is all of these and more. *Parakletos* literally means "one called alongside with sufficient strength." So the Holy Spirit is our Helper, Comforter, Advocate, Intercessor, and Consoler, called alongside us to dwell in us and give us sufficient strength. Sufficient strength for what? To do the works of Jesus and even greater works: "Most assuredly, I say to you, he who believes in Me, the works that I do he will do also; and greater works than these he will do, because I go to My Father (John 14:12).

How is this possible? Remember, John 15:5 says that we can do nothing without Jesus. Yet we are to do the same works He did, and even greater works, even though He is no longer here on the earth with us in person. There is only one way we can do the works of Jesus, not to mention greater works: through the power of the Holy Spirit who indwells us. Jesus said that His Spirit would abide with us forever, that He would dwell with us and be in us (see John 14:16-17).

This means that the Holy Spirit will never depart from us. He is with us wherever we go and in whatever we do. At home, at church, at school, on the job—the Holy Spirit is always with us. In Psalm 139 David wrote:

> *Where can I go from Your Spirit? Or where can I flee from Your presence? If I ascend into heaven, you are there; if I make my bed in hell, behold, You are there. If I take the wings of the morning, and dwell in the*

uttermost parts of the sea, even there Your hand shall lead me, and Your right hand shall hold me (Psalm 139:7-10).

When the Holy Spirit enters our hearts, He enters to stay. There is nowhere we can go where He is not with us. Our Comforter is with us always! Isn't that a comforting thought, especially in these turbulent, unsettling, and uncertain times in which we live?

The Holy Spirit Imparts Spiritual Gifts

Part of the Spirit's ministry as our Helper and the One called alongside for sufficient strength is to impart spiritual gifts to us. Spiritual gifts are not for "superstars" (remember, there are no "superstars" in the Body of Christ) but for every believer. The impartation of Spiritual gifts is a sovereign work of the Spirit; He gives as He chooses to give. Paul provides a perfect description of this ministry of the Spirit:

There are diversities of gifts, but the same Spirit. There are differences of ministries, but the same Lord. And there are diversities of activities, but it is the same God who works all in all. But the manifestation of the Spirit is given to each one for the profit of all: for to one is given the word of wisdom through the Spirit, to another the word of knowledge through the same Spirit, to another faith by the same Spirit, to another gifts of healings by the same Spirit, to another the working of miracles, to another prophecy, to another discerning of spirits, to another different kinds of tongues, to another the interpretation of tongues. But one and the same Spirit works all these things, distributing to each one individually as He wills (1 Corinthians 12:4-11).

The Holy Spirit distributes spiritual gifts to each one individually as He wills. That means just what it says. No matter who you are or how humble your talents, abilities, or education may be, if you are a born-again believer in Jesus Christ, you have been gifted by the Holy Spirit. And He gifts you because He wants to use you. Of course, the greatest spiritual gift of all is the Holy Spirit Himself. As if His continual indwelling presence wasn't enough by itself, He also makes every spiritual gift available to us according to the Spirit's purpose and desire. And that's what we need to remember: spiritual gifts are not for us; they are for the good of the Church and the glory of Christ. Spiritual gifts are not toys for our amusement or blessings, for our comfort and pleasure; they are tools for advancing the Kingdom of God.

One of the purposes of the prophetic gifts—prophecy, words of wisdom, and words of knowledge—is to encourage the Body of Christ and to increase believers' faith. This can occur at either the corporate or individual level. One example we have already seen is the elderly lady I spoke about in Chapter Three, to whom God said that He saw her picking that duck. Let me share a couple more personal examples.

During one meeting, when I was prophesying, a married couple came forward, and as they were standing there, I asked the Lord, "What word do You have for this couple?" He replied, "I want you to look that woman right in the eye and say, 'I don't care if the macaroni's dry.'"

I hesitated. "Now Lord, I thought, "can't you give me a verse or something that will really unlock their hearts and make them know how much you really love them?" He said, "That's my word." So I looked at her and said, "Honey, God says that He doesn't care if the macaroni's dry."

As soon as I said that, she fell to the floor screaming and her husband backed away and started shaking. What was it all about? That very evening, just before they had come to the meeting, they had had a big blow-up at home. She had precooked the macaroni and it had gotten dry, and when her husband got home he threw a regular hissy fit because the macaroni was dry! What was God saying to this couple? He was saying, "I know what goes on at your house. I see what you're really like." The wife knew she was under the watchful eye of God, and the husband knew he was under the judging eye of God. That will certainly give a new perspective to your day!

On another occasion, I was speaking at a conference and suddenly saw in my spirit, just as clearly as if it were right in front of me, a check for $7,227.17. The Lord said to me, "What do you see?" I replied, "Lord, I see a check for $7,227.17." He said, "I want you to announce in this room that somebody is due that check."

So I stopped in the middle of everything and did what the Lord told me to do. I said, "Someone in this room is due a check for $7,227.17. It will be returned to you in the near future."

I could sense the unbelief in the building. I could tell that people were thinking, "Yeah, sure. He made that story up!"

But that wasn't all. There was more to the story. I said, "Here's what happened. The person who owes you this check thinks it has already been paid, but it actually has slid down between the front seat and the console of a vehicle." Talk about going out on a limb!

Nothing more happened that night regarding this word of knowledge. Many weeks later, however, I was back in that same city and a woman came up to me. She asked me, "Do you remember that night in the auditorium when you said a person was going to receive a check?"

"Yes I do," I replied.

Smiling, she pulled out a check stub and there it was: a check for $7,227.17. This lady was a real estate agent, and the man who owed her this commission thought he had paid her. He had taken his Cadillac Escalade to a car dealer to have it detailed in preparation for trading it in, and while the work was being done, someone happened to look between the front seat and the console and found the lady's check. The man promptly sent the check to her along with interest for all the months she was due and it had gone unpaid!

Don't we serve a faithful and a wonderful God?

The Holy Spirit Instructs Us

The Holy Spirit abides in us not only to be our Comforter and to impart spiritual gifts, but also to be our Teacher. He indwells us to instruct us. Jesus said: "But the Helper, the Holy Spirit, whom the Father will send in My name, He will teach you all things, and bring to your remembrance all things that I said to you" (John 14:26).

Again speaking of the Spirit, Jesus promised His disciples:

And when He has come, He will convict the world of sin, and of righteousness, and of judgment: of sin, because they do not believe in Me; of righteousness, because I go to My Father and you see Me no more; of judgment, because the ruler of this world is judged. I still have many things to say to you, but you cannot bear them now. However, when He, the Spirit of truth, has come, He will guide you into all truth; for He will not speak on His own authority, but whatever He hears He will speak; and He will tell you things to come. He will glorify Me, for He will take of what is Mine and declare it to you. All things that the Father has are Mine. Therefore I said that He will take of Mine and declare it to you (John 16:8-15).

How does the Spirit instruct us? In many different ways. Have you ever started to do something that you shouldn't and a little small voice inside says, "Uh, uh, uh, don't do that"? Guess whose voice that is! The Holy Spirit. Quite often, and probably most of the time, He instructs us through a still, small voice. That's why we need to cultivate our spiritual listening skills, so that we can hear the Spirit when He speaks to us.

Another way the Holy Spirit instructs us is by reminding us of the things that Jesus said (see John 14:26). This was particularly true for the apostles. They spent three years with Jesus, yet they often failed to understand what He was trying to teach them. That all changed after they received the Holy Spirit. Through the Spirit's illumination, everything that Jesus had taught by word and example suddenly fell into place. Suddenly, it all made sense. And that which they had seen and heard from Jesus, they passed on faithfully to others through their preaching, their teaching, their miracle-working and, in the case of some, their writing. Of the eight men identified as writers of the New Testament, four were apostles (Matthew, Peter, Paul, and John) and the other four (Mark, Luke, James, and Jude) all had close association with the apostles, with Jesus or with both. The Holy Spirit brought to their remembrance the things Jesus had said to them, gave them understanding of it, and enabled and inspired them to write it all down in an infallible record for all future generations of believers.

For us, the Spirit reminding us of what Jesus said means, in practical terms, bringing to mind a Scripture passage when we need it for a specific situation. In other words, the Spirit helps us apply the Word of God in our daily lives. God's Word is, after all, a living Word, always fresh and always relevant.

The Spirit also instructs us by guiding us into the knowledge of "all truth" (see John 16:13). This means that He gives us discernment to distinguish truth from error. There are a lot of lies, errors, and false teachings flying around in our world, so we must be constantly on our guard against deception. Jesus Himself warned, "For false christs and false prophets will rise and show signs and wonders to deceive, if possible, even the elect" (Mark 13:22). The Holy Spirit is our Instructor of Truth and our Guardian against deception. And He always takes us back to the Word of God—always! This is why Jesus said of the Spirit, "He will not speak on His own authority, but whatever He hears He will speak; and He will tell you things to come. He will glorify Me, for He will take of what is Mine and declare it to you" (John 16:13b-14).

You don't have to be a great scholar to understand spiritual truth. All you need is the Holy Spirit and a willing, submissive heart. The apostle John wrote, "But the anointing which you have received from Him *abides in you*, and you do not need that anyone teach you; but as the same anointing teaches you concerning all things, and is true, and is not a lie, and just as it has taught you, you will abide in Him" (1 John 2:27). As a born again believer, you have a resident Teacher inside of you who is available 24/7, 365 days a year. If you need to know something from the Word of God, you don't have to buy a whole bunch of commentaries. Ask the Holy Spirit to give you understanding. He is the best Bible interpreter of them all.

Don't get me wrong: there is nothing at all wrong with solid, systematic Bible study that takes advantage of the spiritual wisdom and scriptural insights of others. But there is no substitute for going straight to the source. The Bible is its own best commentary and the Spirit its supreme interpreter. As Paul reminded Timothy, "All Scripture is given by inspiration of God, and is profitable for doctrine, for reproof, for correction, for instruction in righteousness, that the man of God may be complete, thoroughly equipped for every good work" (2 Tim. 3:16-17). The Greek word translated *inspiration* here is *theopneustos*, which literally means "divinely breathed." In other words, the Bible came about through the spoken breath of God—through His Spirit. Peter adds, "No prophecy of Scripture is of any private interpretation, for prophecy never came by the will of man, but holy men of God spoke as they were moved by the Holy Spirit" (2 Pet. 1:20b-21). If the Holy Spirit wrote the Bible, He can tell you what it really means. And what does the Bible mean? It means what it says—and it says what it means.

Another way the Holy Spirit instructs us is by giving us assurance of our salvation. He fills our spirits with the confident certainty that we belong to God—that we are members of His family. As Paul told the Christians in Rome, "The Spirit Himself bears witness with our spirit that we are children of God, and if children, then heirs—heirs of God and joint heirs with Christ" (Rom. 8:16-17a). Similarly, he wrote to the Galatians: "And because you are sons, God has sent forth the Spirit of His Son into your hearts, crying out, 'Abba, Father!' Therefore you are no longer a slave but a son, and if a son, then an heir of God through Christ" (Gal. 4:6-7). *Abba* is a term of endearment that is less formal and more intimate than *father*. Its English equivalent would be *Daddy* or *Papa*. That's how close to God we can be through the Holy Spirit, and it is the Spirit who teaches us about that relationship. He encourages us to draw near to the Father with a heart full of assurance.

The Holy Spirit is our Teacher and our Guide. He indwells us to instruct us. And He wants to pour His anointing out upon a hungry, desperate people. He wants to teach us and then show us who we are in Christ.

The Holy Spirit Teaches Us How to Pray

Jesus gave us a "model" prayer (see Matt. 6:9-13), but it is the Holy Spirit who teaches us to pray. The Spirit also gives us confidence that our prayers will be answered. John affirmed this truth when he wrote: "Now this is the confidence that we have in Him, that if we ask anything according to His will, He hears us. And if we know that He hears us, whatever we ask, we know that we have the petitions that we have asked of Him" (1 John 5:14-15).

What's the key to having our prayers answered? To pray according to God's will. And how do we know God's will? Through the Holy Spirit. Paul said that, as Christians, we have the mind of Christ (see 1 Cor. 2:16), and the Holy Spirit works to bring our thoughts into alignment with Christ's thoughts so that we can know and do His will. But the Spirit's work on our behalf in prayer goes even farther. He helps us pray when we don't know how or what to pray:

> *Likewise the Spirit also helps in our weaknesses. For we do not know what we should pray for as we ought, but the Spirit Himself makes intercession for us with groanings which cannot be uttered. Now He who searches the hearts knows what the mind of the Spirit is, because He makes intercession for the saints according to the will of God* (Romans 8:26-27).

So the Spirit not only teaches us how to pray, He also intercedes on our behalf. If we fill our hearts with the Word of God as the Spirit instructs us and pray as the Spirit leads us, we will never go amiss in our prayers. We will always receive God's answer because we will always pray according to His will. From the Word of God, we will learn the promises of God, which we can then pray back to Him. God loves it when we pray His own promises back to Him—when we take Him at His Word. To remind God of what He said is not presumption on our part; it is an expression of our faith. It shows that God is the One whom we turn to and on whom we depend.

The Holy Spirit's ministry in prayer, then, is to get our hearts and minds in tune with the heart and mind of God. It's like there's this great tuning fork in Heaven, resonating with the heart of God, and God wants His children on earth to resonate at the same frequency. That's what happens in our lives when the Spirit aligns our hearts to the will and purpose of God. He brings us into synchronization with the heart of the Father.

Jesus said that it is the Father's pleasure to give us the Kingdom (see Luke 12:32). If the Father has given us the Kingdom, that means that we have access to all the riches and resources of the Kingdom. Prayer is one of the keys that un-locks the doors to Kingdom resources. Righteous living is an-other. Do you want to receive more from God, not to consume on your own lusts but to use for His glory? Then ask Him. James 4:2b says, "You do not have because you do not ask." If you are not seeing much from God, it may be because you are not expecting much from God. William Carey, the first Baptist missionary to India, said, "Expect great things from God, at-tempt great things for God." That is wise counsel for prayer as well as for life. Don't be afraid to ask for big things.

Elisha was a man with a big vision. For years he served as assistant to the prophet Elijah. Shortly before Elijah was taken to Heaven in a fiery chariot, he told Elisha to ask for whatever he wanted. Elisha said, "I want a double portion of your anointing." That was a bold request, because Elijah was the most highly anointed prophet of his day. Yet, God fulfilled Elisha's request (see 2 Kings 2:9-14). He is always looking for people with a big vision. Elisha did receive a double portion of the anointing that had rested on Elijah. The Bible indicates that Elisha did exactly double the number of miracles that Elijah did. Elisha received big because he asked big—and be-cause he believed big. The Holy Spirit can teach us to do both.

Abiding in the Anointing

The Bible says that the Holy Spirit abides in us. But abid-ing is a two-way street. It is just as important for us to abide in the Spirit, because apart from Him we can do nothing. If we do not abide in the Spirit, we cannot walk in the anointing. When we abide in the Spirit and in the anointing, we abide in the continuing presence of the Lord. It is this real and tangible presence of God with us that sets us apart from the rest of the world. And the world can't help but notice.

When Peter and John were brought before the Jewish high council for "illegally" preaching Jesus and for healing a lame man, it quickly became obvious to these Jewish religious leaders that something was different about these two men: "Now when they saw the boldness of Peter and John, and perceived that they were uneducated and untrained men, they marveled. And they realized that they had been with Jesus" (Acts 4:13). What made Peter and John so bold as to preach Christ fearlessly to the very men most responsible for His crucifixion? They walked in the anointing, and that made the difference.

Be warned: if you walk in the anointing, it will mark you for life! People who come around you will know that you have "been with Jesus." But isn't that what you want? Don't you want people to know you have been in the presence of the Lord? Don't you want His presence to shine brightly in your life? After all, the living presence of God in us as believers is what makes us unique in the world. And God wants us to be unique. We are supposed to be different. We are supposed to be in the world but not of the world. We are supposed to confront our culture with the eternal claims of the gospel of Christ, not to conform to our culture. To do all these things, we must abide in the anointing.

Here's another warning: abide in the anointing, because if you're not careful, the very thing that got you there will carry you away. When you get the anointing, people will be drawn to you. It will be easy to become so busy that you will forget to be still and get into the Lord's presence. People ask me often, "Bobby, how do you travel all over the world, keep such a busy schedule, and still walk in the anointing?" The answer? I've learned how to tune people out when necessary. I can be on a plane with dozens of other people and just zone in on the Lord. Part of the ministry of the Holy Spirit is to help you lay aside distractions, get quiet, be still, and focus on Christ.

Psalm 91 paints a beautiful picture of abiding in the Lord:

He who dwells in the secret place of the Most High shall abide under the shadow of the Almighty. I will say of the Lord, "He is my refuge and my fortress; My God, in Him I will trust." Surely He shall deliver you from the snare of the fowler and from the perilous pestilence. He shall cover you with His feathers, and under His wings you shall take refuge; His truth shall be your shield and buckler. You shall not be afraid of the terror by night, nor of the arrow that flies by day, nor of the pestilence that walks in darkness, nor of the destruction that lays waste at noonday.... Because you have made the Lord, who is my refuge, even the Most High, your dwelling place, no evil shall befall you, nor shall any plague come near your dwelling; for He shall give His angels charge over you, to keep you in all your ways. In their hands they shall bear you up, lest you dash your foot against a stone (Psalm 91:1-6;9-12).

I was in the Mojave Desert once and saw a light pole sticking up. The sun was high in the sky, it was extremely hot, and that light pole cast a tiny shadow. Yet inside that shadow rested a roadrunner and a lizard, hiding from the heat of the day. They were abiding in the shadow of that light pole. If animals have the sense to abide in the shadow, why don't we?

A shadow is always connected to the substance. The key to walking in the anointing is learning to "abide under the shadow of the Almighty." Under His shadow there is peace. Under His shadow there is safety. Under His shadow there is rest. Under His shadow there is His divine Presence. Under His shadow...that's where I want to be. Don't you?

CHAPTER H

Walking in Victory

When I was growing up in the sand hills of east Texas, times were very difficult for our family. By the time I was four years old, my father had died in a mental institution as the result of a sexually transmitted disease that destroyed his mind. My dear mother was attempting to raise three children with no husband and almost no money. She took in as much washing and ironing as she could just to put food on the table. We were dirt poor in the truest sense of the word.

My siblings and I were "stair-step" children. I was the youngest. Kay, my sister, was two years older than me, and my brother Glenn, one year older. Adding to the difficulty of those years, Glenn had been born with crumbling of the hipbones and was crippled, unable to walk without crutches. I still remember how I used to pull him around in a red wagon. It seemed that if Glenn had any hope of walking ever, he needed medical help that our mother simply could not afford.

One day, when I was four years old, I was outside playing when I heard a voice in my head speak in an extremely clear voice, "Don't get on that pony!" I didn't know anything about any pony, and I also didn't know anything about the voice in my head, so I said out loud, "What pony?" It was at that point that I suddenly felt like my entire body had been shocked with electricity that froze me in my tracks. I heard the voice again, not in my head this time but right in front of me. It was an audible voice that I heard with my ears: "Don't get on that pony!"

The moment I was able to move again, I ran into the house, into my room, and jumped in my bed. My brother said, "What's wrong with you?"

"Don't get on that pony!" I replied.

"What pony?" Glenn asked.

I said, "I don't know, just don't get on that pony!"

For the next several days, every time I got still, the same voice would speak to me, reminding me not to get on the pony.

A few days later my mother put some of Glenn's clothes and mine in a box and fixed up a picnic lunch. My uncle drove up in a big, shiny car. He opened the trunk and Mother put the box of clothes in. Then she put Glenn and me in the back seat, got in the front seat with our uncle and off we drove.

As a four-year-old boy, it was exciting to sit in the back seat of this big car and watch as we drove through one small town after another. At one point, we even stopped at a distant roadside park and ate our picnic lunch. I was very happy to be going on a trip, but even as young as I was, I couldn't help but notice that my mother did not seem very happy.

After hours of driving, we finally pulled up in front of a large ranch house. As our uncle parked the car, Glenn and I strained our necks to see what was going on and where we were.

Suddenly, from around the corner of the big building came a woman leading a small pony. She was carrying two cowboy hats and some toy pistols. My uncle opened our car door as the woman approached. The first words out of her mouth were, "Hello boys. Get on the pony, and let's take a ride!"

My eyes grew wide from shock, and I slid all the way over to the other side of the seat next to Glenn, and we both started screaming, "I ain't getting on that pony! I ain't getting on that pony!"

That's when our mother began crying and said, "I just can't do it. I will not do it." She told our uncle, "Turn this car around, and take us home."

Later I learned that they had taken us to an orphanage that eased the separation of children from their families by distracting them with a pony ride.

How I praise God today for speaking to a little boy with a strong warning that helped keep a struggling family together! God is so good! Nahum 1:7 says, "The Lord is good, a stronghold in the day of trouble." This verse echoes Psalm 46:1: "God is our refuge and strength, a very present help in trouble."

If God was concerned about keeping a dirt-poor Texas family together, He certainly cares about you and your situation, whatever it may be. And if He could work in our family to bring us victory over all the obstacles and circumstances that threatened to pull us apart, He can also enable you to walk in victory all the days of your life. For every true, born-again believer, final victory is assured on the Day of the Lord, when Christ returns to receive His own, but victory can also be ours between now and then if we focus on a few fundamental principles.

Advance with Boldness

Our first step toward victory is to advance with boldness. The Spirit of God is encouraging each of us to advance. Like Joshua, we are commanded to be "strong and very courageous" (see Josh. 1:7) as we move in power to take the Kingdom for the King! This is a season of no compromise for the Body of Christ! We are to walk with clean hands and pure hearts, drawing ever closer to our Lord. The cry has gone forth: "No hesitation!" We must rise up, walking in dominion power and laying hold of the promises of God. This is not a time to be weak and waffling but rather a time to be extremely bold and brave. Whatever the Lord has called us to do, He will not leave us alone to do in our own strength. He will empower us and go before us, just as He went before the Israelites in a pillar of cloud by day and a pillar of fire by night (see Exod. 13:21).

Listen with your whole heart. Take courage! God has promised victory! He has called you to be the head and not the tail (see Deut. 28:13). Victory is yours because His power is greater than the world's power: "You are of God, little children, and have overcome them, because He who is in you is greater than he who is in the world" (1 John 4:4). You were created for victory; now is the time to shake yourself and declare the proclamation found in Micah 3:8a: "Truly I am full of power by the Spirit of the Lord"!

We are in the harvest of the end of the ages, when both the seeds of good and evil are coming to full fruit. The Kingdom of Heaven suffers violence and the violent take it by force (see Matt. 11:12). God is calling us to arise and take a strong stand against the works of darkness. We are to take the land, and this victory will be accomplished by individuals as well as by the Church, the corporate Body of Christ. The end-time Church will be a people of demonstrated power (see 1 Cor. 2:1-5). It is time for the world to see a true demonstration of the power of God's Spirit. The cry has come up before the throne of God, "Oh, that You would rend the heavens! That you would come down!" (Isa. 64:1a).

Join with the plea of Psalm 90:16-17: "Let Your work appear to Your servants, and Your glory to their children. And let the beauty of the Lord our God be upon us, and establish the work of our hands for us; yes, establish the work of our hands." The Church should be hungry and desperate to see the works of the Lord. We should long for Him to establish the works of our hands—His work in the world. I don't know about you, but I am weary of seeing the plans and purposes of men; I long to see the mighty acts of God! The Spirit of Truth is calling for us to come into the presence of the Lord.

The way is clear. Any believer can advance higher. God has extended an open invitation for all who will to "Come up here" (see Rev. 4:1), to enter the door that is standing open in Heaven so that we can see more clearly and hear more plainly. Doing so will equip us to advance ever deeper in the anointing, making the most of our divine call.

Paul instructed us to "walk circumspectly, not as fools but as wise, redeeming the time, because the days are evil" (Eph. 5:15-16). This means to walk with the clear goal and aim of fulfilling God's divine purpose. This is not a time for us to wander around the mountain of defeat and unbelief. No! We are to lay hold of the promise of God, take Him at His word, and stand firm in our faith.

One day God released to me this very encouraging statement: "This will be the season when My people begin to believe what they know. My word will move from the head to the heart to the hands." We will become doers of the Word, not content simply to be hearers. God has destined us to walk in victory, not defeat. We are called to be overcomers, not to be overcome. Remember, God has promised that no weapon formed against you can prosper (see Isa. 54:17).

Today the Body of Christ stands poised on the verge of the greatest move of God in the history of mankind. Accordingly, each of us should expect swift and radical change, swift and sure shifting. We do not have the time for another trip around the mountain; we must enter into the promises of God. No matter how confused and confounded we have been in the past, we now can personally begin to cease from our wilderness wanderings and begin to walk in our purpose of seeking first the Kingdom of God (see Matt. 6:33).

Paul prayed that we would "walk worthy of the Lord, fully pleasing Him, being fruitful in every good work and increasing in the knowledge of God" (Col. 1:10). Our highest goal must be to advance the King in His Kingdom. Our prayer each day must be, "Your will be done on earth as it is in Heaven." There must come a swift synchronization of our walk to Heaven's will. Just as Christ could say, "I only do that which I see My Father doing" (see John 5:19) we too must have clear focus. No higher commendation could be given than hearing our Father declare, "Well done, good and faithful servant; you were faithful over a few things, I will make you ruler over many things. Enter into the joy of your Lord" (Matt. 25:21).

It is imperative that we maintain a deep walk in the Word of God. This will bring about the freedom that we need to draw near to the Lord. We must approach His hill with clean hands and a pure heart (see Ps. 24:4-6). Each day we must seek to draw ever nearer to Christ, seeking to yield our wills ever more to His will. It is as we truly behold Him with an unveiled face that we are changed into His likeness (see 2 Cor. 3:18.).

The blood of Christ has power to set mankind free from all bondage; the choice is ours, if we want to walk in freedom. In the days to come, we will see a radical return to the message of the redemptive blood of Christ, which is able to cleanse all sin.

Christ is calling His Church today to advance on every front: to walk in the Word, in His anointing, and in His power to overthrow the gates of hell and set the captives free.

Obey the Lord

The second key principle to walking in victory is to walk in obedience. Obey the Lord. It's that simple. Many ask the question, "Why do so many believers live in a state of bondage and defeat?" One of the main reasons is that they (we) have left their (our) first love. If this is the case, our first prayer must be a prayer of confession and repentance. Then our second prayer must be, "Lord, restore my passion for You!" Christ has provided overwhelming victory for us through His blood. Therefore, there is no need—or excuse—for us to continue living in defeat. Victory, however, will require our dedication to overcoming strongholds. If we will reaffirm our faith and rededicate ourselves to radical obedience, we can leave defeat in the dust and start walking in life-long victory.

Remember the words of that old gospel hymn that says it so well:

Trust and obey,
For there's no other way
To be happy in Jesus,
But to trust and obey.[1]

One of the most important aspects of the Christian walk is learning to obey quickly the voice of the Spirit of God. Remember, just hearing the Word (voice) of the Lord is not enough; doing it is what matters. Obedience assures us victory in the long run, even if we experience setbacks and hardships at times. Victory will be ours because the Victorious One abides within us.

The word *obey* is one of the strongest words in human language to indicate hearing. Obeying the voice of Jesus is the only true evidence that we have heard Him. If we do not obey, we might as well be deaf; the result is the same. In fact, lack of obedience is evidence of lack of faith. James said that faith without works is dead (see James 2:26), and Jesus warned, "Not everyone who says to Me, 'Lord, Lord,' shall enter the kingdom of Heaven, but he who *does* the will of My Father in Heaven" (Matt. 7:21). True faith is always revealed in obedience, which is why the word in the New Testament that is usually translated *faith* also means *faithfulness*. Our faithfulness is measured by the degree of our obedience to our "prime directive" from Christ: "But seek first the Kingdom of God and His righteousness; and all these things shall be added to you" (Matt. 6:33).

Sad to say, many Christians have spent too much of their lives in disorientation and defeat because they simply have not obeyed the Word of God. It is as we seek first the Kingdom and righteousness of God—His priorities—that we receive clear guidance and revelation, not to mention provision for all the practical necessities of life that the rest of the world sweats and labors and worries over.

One source of many believers' confusion is that they try to walk in the light of their own sparks rather than in the light of God's revealed Word. They make vital decisions based on their own desires and other earthly, temporary matters instead of seeking first the purposes of God's Kingdom. If we would base all of our decisions on seeking the purposes of His Kingdom first, everything else would be added to us—without struggle or stress. That's the force of the Lord's promise in Matthew 6:33. We would have nothing to be anxious about, knowing who our

Source and Protector is. Obedience is the key to everything, but we must obey the right things: the will and Word of God.

There is no greater freedom, no greater peace, than that which results from living our lives dedicated to the Lord in all things. No matter what your past has been like, let your past stay in the past. God created you to be the head and not the tail. His plan is for you to be above and not below. Now is the time to walk in freedom, and freedom is found in obedience.

Sow Righteous Seed

Walking in victory also depends on our sowing righteous seed every day. In clear view from my back door in the beautiful Blue Ridge Mountains of North Carolina is a huge apple orchard covering several hundred acres. What a joy it is to watch the trees bloom in the spring and bear delicious fruit in the fall. All this is the result of one man with a big dream. John Chapman, also known as Johnny Appleseed, came through our region in Moravian Falls, North Carolina, using the apple to preach the gospel. He used to say that you could count the seeds in an apple but that you could not count the apples in a seed. This whole region of the state is now covered in apple trees that supposedly originated from this evangelist who preached here more than two hundred years ago.

Like Johnny Appleseed, you too have precious seeds to sow—a special grace gift from God. What seed is the Lord leading you to sow that will provide a harvest? Do not miss your opportunity to sow, or you will miss your opportunity to celebrate at harvest time. Your joy in the Lord will be proportional to your investment in the Lord. Sow little and you reap little; sow much and you reap abundantly. This law of sowing and reaping includes, but is not limited to, our use of money. According to Scripture, every Christian's life should have such an overflow that we can be a channel of blessing to all who are in need. This is what Paul had in mind when he wrote to the Corinthians:

But this I say: He who sows sparingly will also reap sparingly, and he who sows bountifully will also reap bountifully. So let each one give as he purposes in his heart, not grudgingly or of necessity; for God loves a cheerful giver. And God is able to make all grace abound toward you, that you, always having all sufficiency in all things, may have an abundance for every good work. As it is written: "He has dispersed abroad, He has given to the poor; His righteousness endures forever." Now may He who supplies seed to the sower, and bread for food, supply and multiply the seed you have sown and increase the fruits of your righteousness, while you are enriched in everything for all liberality, which causes thanksgiving through us to God (2 Corinthians 9:6-11).

This is a part of our "Promised Land": having such an abundance, so much more than we ourselves need, that it blesses and touches every one around us. I'm not just talking about money or material goods but also about faith, hope, love, healing, and every other dimension of life. But it begins with material things because, as the Lord Jesus said, we cannot be trusted with the true riches of the Kingdom if we do not learn how to handle earthly riches (see Luke 16:11).

Even so, Christ's Kingdom is not of this world, and neither are the true blessings of the Promised Land that we are seeking. They are something that we are to walk in and demonstrate in this life, but they are not of this world.

Many are not able to hear such things, believing them to be "negative" prophecies, but they are biblical prophecies. Even the rough times that lie ahead will not be very difficult for those who have built their houses on the Rock by hearing and obeying the words of the Lord. On the other hand, difficult days lie ahead for those who do not abide in Christ. The fear barometer is going to rise a few more points because the earth is going to be groaning and travailing, and the lawless are going to become even more ruthless.

People who have given themselves over to darkness will fall into even greater darkness. As the darkness grows, however, the light of the glory of the Lord, which is coming upon His people, will grow even brighter, eventually dispersing the darkness entirely, until the earth is "filled with the knowledge of the glory of the Lord, as the waters cover the sea" (Hab. 2:14).

I believe that as we advance in the Spirit, in these days that lie ahead, we will move closer and closer to the time when the prophecy of Isaiah will be fulfilled in the Body of Christ, just as it was first fulfilled with the coming of Jesus Himself:

> *Arise, shine; for your light has come! And the glory of the Lord is risen upon you. For behold, the darkness shall cover the earth, and deep darkness the people; but the Lord will arise over you, and His glory will be seen upon you. The Gentiles shall come to your light, and kings to the brightness of your rising. Lift up your eyes all around, and see: they all gather together, they come to you; your sons shall come from afar, and your daughters shall be nursed at your side. Then you shall see and become radiant, and your heart shall swell with joy; because the abundance of the sea shall be turned to you, the wealth of the Gentiles shall come to you* (Isaiah 60:1-5).

We see here that, at the very time that "deep darkness" is coming upon the people of the earth, the glory of the Lord is coming upon His people. If we are building our lives on the

Kingdom of God, which cannot be shaken, we will have nothing to fear from the things that are now coming and are soon to come upon the world. Rather, it will be a time for great rejoicing when the glory of the Lord appears upon His people. The greatest treasure that we could ever possess is the one we already have—the Lord with us. Great days and unparalleled opportunities lie ahead, so we must plan ahead by taking advantage of every chance that we have to sow good seeds of righteousness now.

Respect Authority

Any believer who desires to walk in the anointing and experience on-going victory in daily living will have a proper and biblical respect for authority. First, we acknowledge Christ as Lord—Master—and as Head of His Body, the Church. That means that He has authority over us and that we are responsible to obey Him. Respect for authority and obedience go hand in hand. The Holy Spirit is always working to mold us and make us more like Jesus. He is preparing us to fulfill God's purpose, the establishment of His Kingdom. The more we learn about the King and His Kingdom, the more we will learn the importance of respecting authority.

A Kingdom is the realm that is under the king's authority. To be entrusted with authority from the Lord requires that one first be under the authority of the Lord. We must also willingly submit to the authority of those spiritual leaders that the Lord has placed over us. Unless we learn proper respect for authority, rules, and order in the Body of Christ, we will be a great danger to ourselves and others if we are given—or grab—more authority. This definitely flies in the face of the way the world operates, and as we move closer to the Day of the Lord, we can expect this contrast to increase.

Authority, discipline, and rules are not necessarily legalism, although in the wrong hands they can cross that line. In all my years in ministry, I have never yet met one person who carries significant spiritual authority who was not at some time subjected either to an extreme form of legalism or to some other form of overly controlling authority.

One of the great examples of this in Scripture is King David. King Saul was the tool that God used to fashion David into the great king that he would become. How did David react to the authority in his life that was so unjust and had even been demonized? David honored Saul to the end, refusing to lift his own hand against the king, even after Saul had tried to kill him many times (see 1 Sam. 24; 26). David even rewarded the men who recovered Saul's body and gave him a proper burial. He then went to the completely unprecedented extreme of honoring Saul's remaining family (see 2 Sam. 2:1-7; 9:1-13). This was the exact opposite of the way of kings in those times, who quickly slew the children of any rivals. But David was of a different spirit.

It was David's great respect for authority, those who were "anointed of the Lord," that enabled the Lord to entrust him with such remarkable authority that he was even used to establish the throne that the King of Kings would sit upon. The Lord Jesus Himself would be affectionately called "the Son of David."

With David as our shining example of the way to respect authority, let us consider these exhortations from Scripture concerning authority:

> *Let every soul be subject to the governing authorities. For there is no authority except from God, and the authorities that exist are appointed by God. Therefore whoever resists the authority resists the ordinance of God, and those who resist will bring judgment on themselves. For rulers are not a terror to good works, but to evil. Do you want to be unafraid of the*

authority? Do what is good, and you will have praise from the same. For he is God's minister to you for good. But if you do evil, be afraid; for he does not bear the sword in vain; for he is God's minister, an avenger to execute wrath on him who practices evil. Therefore you must be subject, not only because of wrath but also for conscience' sake. For because of this you also pay taxes, for they are God's ministers attending continually to this very thing. Render therefore to all their due: taxes to whom taxes are due, customs to whom customs, fear to whom fear, honor to whom honor (Romans 13:1-7).

It is worth remembering that the highest authority in Paul's world, at the time that he wrote these words, was Nero, who was one of the most corrupt, evil, and demented of the Caesars and the one who eventually ordered Paul's execution. Nowhere does it say to be in subjection only to the most righteous and just authorities, but rather to all authorities.

Many Christians today disqualify themselves from receiving more authority from God because of the way they disrespect civil authority in its many and diverse manifestations. Remember, it was because of David's high calling that he was subjected to such a great test with a cruel, demented king like Saul. If you want to walk in great authority, learn first to walk humbly, faithfully, and obediently under authority.

A Better Way

There is an erosion of respect for authority taking place in our times. It seems to be fast becoming a veritable meltdown. This will happen before the end of this age, and it will be the primary cause for "the great time of trouble" or "the great tribulation" (see Matt. 24:21). However, regardless of how outrageous governments or the authorities become, those who will be trusted with the authority of the coming Kingdom must in every way treat them with dignity and respect. This is "the Saul test."

Do not speak evil of your leaders. Do not disrespect the police, mayors, governors, or any others in authority, and teach respect for them to your children, beginning with respect for their teachers, principals, etc. This does not mean that we cannot disagree with their policies or actions, and in the cases of teachers, this might include some of their teachings, but we must do it in the most respectful way possible. In First Timothy, Paul gives us a more positive approach to authority: "First of all, then, I urge that entreaties and prayers, petitions and thanksgivings, be made on behalf of all men, for kings and all who are in authority, in order that we may lead a tranquil and quiet life in all godliness and dignity" (1 Tim. 2:1 2 NASB).

Here Paul exhorts us to pray first of all for those in authority. In other words, it should be our primary prayer activity.

In contrast to the growing lawlessness, there is an emerging generation of spiritual leaders who will come forth in the opposite spirit. These are the ones who will preach the gospel of the Kingdom with power because they will have been found trustworthy to handle spiritual authority.

It was the Gentile centurion who understood the nature of authority and how having authority happened by being under authority. The Lord commended him as having greater faith than anyone that He had found in Israel (see Matt. 8:5-10). This is what we must understand if we are going to be trusted with the authority, which the Lord will give only to the trustworthy.

Before we consider a few simple things that we can do to combat this growing lawlessness, let us take time to think about what the Lord said about it in the following Scriptures:

Many will say to Me on that day, "Lord, Lord, did we not prophesy in Your name, and in Your name cast out demons, and in Your name perform many miracles?" And then I will declare to them, "I never knew you; depart from Me, you who practice lawlessness" (Matthew 7:22-23 NASB)

No matter what type of gift we manifest or how spiritual and righteous we sound, if we do not truly know and follow the Lord, we will be rejected.

In another place, Jesus gives another stern warning that is extremely clear: "The Son of Man will send forth His angels, and they will gather out of His kingdom all stumbling blocks, and those who commit lawlessness, and will cast them into the furnace of fire; in that place there shall be weeping and gnashing of teeth" (Matt. 13:41-42 NASB).

Harsh judgment will be rendered upon those who place stumbling blocks in the path of other followers or in the path of those who wish to follow, as well as upon those who commit lawlessness.

Particularly distasteful to the Lord are those who cloak their lawlessness in religious garb:

Woe to you, scribes and Pharisees, hypocrites! For you are like whitewashed tombs which on the outside appear beautiful, but inside they are full of dead men's bones and all uncleanness. So you too outwardly appear righteous to men, but inwardly you are full of hypocrisy and lawlessness (Matthew 23:27-28 NASB).

Even in the midst of rampant lawlessness, however, there is hope for the faithful: "Because lawlessness is increased, most people's love will grow cold. But the one who endures to the end, he will be saved" (Matt. 24:12-13).

Overcoming Lawlessness

Freedom does not mean that we are to live loose. What then must we do? First, we must understand that although we are not under the law, neither are we above it. We must submit ourselves to the Lord and respect His authority.

As leaders, we must teach our children to do the same. If we do not teach our children to respect authority, we are not equipping them for what will, in all probability, be the major battle they will have to face in these times. Remember why Abraham, the "father of faith," was chosen by God, as Genesis 18:19 tells us: "For I have chosen him, so that he may command his children and his household after him to keep the way of the Lord by doing righteousness and justice, so that the Lord may bring upon Abraham what He has spoken about him" (Genesis 18:19 NASB).

God said that He had chosen Abraham so that he would "command his children...after him to keep the way of the Lord." The very right of parents to exercise authority over their children is under increasing attack in these times. We must prevail in this fight, for the sake of our children. It is essential, however, that we do this in love rather than frustration, anger, or impatience.

We must also understand that sin is lawlessness, and impurity leads to lawlessness, as Paul tells us in Romans:

> *I am speaking in human terms because of the weakness of your flesh. For just as you presented your members as slaves to impurity and to lawlessness, resulting in further lawlessness, so now present your members as slaves to righteousness, resulting in sanctification. For when you were slaves of sin, you were free in regard to righteousness. Therefore what benefit were you then deriving from the things of which you are now ashamed? For the outcome of those things is death. But*

now having been freed from sin and enslaved to God, you derive your benefit, resulting in sanctification, and the outcome, eternal life. For the wages of sin is death, but the free gift of God is eternal life in Christ Jesus our Lord (Romans 6:19-23 NASB).

Lawlessness, like faith, usually begins with a seed, which is then watered and cultivated, bringing forth sin, as described above. It often begins with impurity, which will always lead to lawlessness. Impurity and lawlessness are bound together, as John describes: "And everyone who has this hope fixed on Him purifies himself, just as He is pure. Everyone who practices sin also practices lawlessness; and sin is lawlessness (1 John 3:3-4 NASB).

Finally, let us consider how we can comply with the exhortation of Romans 13:8-14, which follows Paul's exhortation to honor those who are in positions of authority:

Owe nothing to anyone except to love one another; for he who loves his neighbor has fulfilled the law. For this, "You shall not commit adultery, you shall not murder, you shall not steal, you shall not covet," and if there is any other commandment, it is summed up in this saying, "you shall love your neighbor as yourself." Love does no wrong to a neighbor; love therefore is the fulfillment of the law. Do this, knowing the time, that it is already the hour for you to awaken from sleep; for now salvation is nearer to us than when we believed. The night is almost gone, and the day is near. Therefore let us lay aside the deeds of darkness and put on the armor of light. Let us behave properly as in the day, not in carousing and drunkenness, not in sexual promiscuity and sensuality, not in strife and jealousy. But put on the Lord Jesus Christ, and make no provision for the flesh in regard to its lusts (Romans 13:8-14 NASB).

Love, Not Legalism

God's response to lawlessness and rebellion is not legalism, but love. If we are growing in our love for God and for others, it will be the desire of our hearts to keep our hearts pure for them. Love is the fulfillment of the law, and love should be our motivation for teaching our children to love God and to respect authority.

This is such a crucial issue in our times. The Church is in desperate need of true shepherds who have the Father's heart for His people, but few have been willing to submit to the process required to conform their hearts to His. Do not waste the trials that come to you in whatever form—in the Church or in non-Church relationships with people at your job, in your family, within the civil government, etc. Like David, resolve to honor all who are in authority, and do not let bitterness or rejection find a place in your heart. Ephesians 4:32 says, "Be kind to one another, tenderhearted, forgiving one another, even as God in Christ forgave you."

Don't worry that you're not a Christian "superstar." There's no such thing anyway. Those who walk in a powerful anointing are ordinary folks like you and me who got hungry and desperate for a fresh touch from the Lord and humbly submitted themselves to Him. Consequently, God has taken them in their ordinariness and humility and weakness, and He does extraordinary things through them.

And He wants to do the same with you. Submit yourself humbly to God. Advance boldly. Obey the Lord. Sow righteous seeds. Respect authority. Live righteously. Walk in these things, and not only will you walk in a powerful anointing, but you also will walk in victory all the days of your life!

Note

1. John H. Sammis, "Trust and Obey," 1887.

Author Contact Information

BOBBY CONNER
Eagles View Ministries

PO Box 933
Bullard, TX 75757

Website: www.bobbyconner.org

Other teachings by Bobby Conner

BOOKS

SHEPHERD'S ROD 2000

The color this year is going to be black. Meeting God in thick darkness. Y2K is part of God's judgment against our so-called worldly wisdom. Money will be misplaced and food will be in short supply. God is saying to our world: turn or burn.

SHEPHERD'S ROD 2001

As the company of the Prophets begins to walk together, schools of the Prophets will come forth. Study the north gate.

God is releasing a fresh anointing on ears and eyes. Christians are busy observing gifts while God is inspecting fruit.

SHEPHERD'S ROD 2002

This is almost word-for-word the same as Master's Plan.

SHEPHERD'S ROD VOL X

Revelations received in 1999. Lots of judgments. Apostolic leadership emerging will provide a pillar of cloud over the Body. Prophets will be as a flame of fire at night displaying awesome power and miracles. Kingdom keys are being released.

SHEPHERD'S ROD VOL XI

Bobby's revelations received on the Day of Atonement. A time of intense shaking is coming. Stand guard over your household with the Sword of the Spirit. Expect breakthroughs in inventions. The Lord will bring about a Divine Alliance.

ALTAR OF INCENSE

Lord, teach us to pray. True prayer is not the pressure of a man-made ritual, but the pleasure of a relationship. The gap between Heaven and earth is becoming smaller. Satan infiltrates the ranks of intercessors. Pray until something happens. The five ingredients of incense.

UNCTION TO FUNCTION

God's release of Apostolic and Prophetic power for His purposes. It's crucial to have an understanding of your authority. Expect great exploits. Think big.

EMBRACE THE FIRE

Our God is a consuming fire. The flame is not for punishment but for purifying. The fire produces mighty miracles. People are going to be overwhelmed with the nature and character of God. We must be formed in the secret place. (Much like Master's Plan.)

THE STORY OF RUTH

MASTER'S PLAN

God's original intent was that man be conformed into His image. Church leaders have instead worked to form men into their image. Divine union with Christ will produce His divine nature. We need purging and pruning.

UNDERSTANDING THE ANOINTING

Information on general and specific anointings. Bobby Conner was instructed to have Benny Hinn lay hands on him to receive the same anointing. How to receive the anointing. What is the anointing? How do we get it? The results of the anointing.

BOOKLETS

"LET FREEDOM RING"

Obedience and liberty and freedom from fear. Freedom is released by obedience.

"THE CROSS"

Bobby's spiritual experience of being transported back to Jesus' crucifixion.

CDs

- ❖ Third Day Generation: The Release of God's Promises
- ❖ The Story of Ruth
- ❖ Third Day Generation: Demonstration of God's Power
- ❖ Stormy Winds
- ❖ Shepherd's Rod Vol. VIII
- ❖ Approaching the Ancient of Days

FIVE CD SERIES

- ❖ Keys to the Anointing
- ❖ The Ministry of the Spirit
- ❖ Recovering the Anointing
- ❖ Who Shall Ascend
- ❖ God Has Anointed You

DVDs

- ❖ The Power of the Prophetic Word
- ❖ Ears to Hear
- ❖ Conviction vs. Condemnation
- ❖ A Time to Advance
- ❖ Called from Birth

❖ Bobby's Testimony

❖ Hidden Manna

Though we live in dark days, Bobby Conner emphasizes that our source of light will be the spirit of wisdom and revelation, God's hidden manna.

Additional copies of this book and other
book titles from DESTINY IMAGE are
available at your local bookstore.

Call toll-free: 1-800-722-6774.

Send a request for a catalog to:

Destiny Image® Publishers, Inc.
P.O. Box 310
Shippensburg, PA 17257-0310

*"Speaking to the Purposes of God for this
Generation and for the Generations to Come."*

**For a complete list of our titles,
visit us at www.destinyimage.com.**